MODERN WORLD LEADERS

# The Saudi Royal Family

## MODERN WORLD LEADERS

MODERN WORLD LEADERS

# The Saudi Royal Family

Jennifer Bond Reed

With additional text by Brenda Lange

**CHELSEA HOUSE**
PUBLISHERS

An imprint of Infobase Publishing

**The Saudi Royal Family**

Copyright © 2007 by Infobase Publishing

All rights reserved. No part of this book may be reproduced or utilized in any form or by any means, electronic or mechanical, including photocopying, recording, or by any information storage or retrieval systems, without permission in writing from the publisher. For information, contact:

Chelsea House
An imprint of Infobase Publishing
132 West 31st Street
New York, NY 10001

**Library of Congress Cataloging-in-Publication Data**

Reed, Jennifer.
   The Saudi royal family / Jennifer Bond Reed.
      p. cm. — (Modern world leaders)
   Originally published: Philadelphia: Chelsea House Publishers, 2003,
in series: Major world leaders.
   Includes bibliographical references and index.
   ISBN 0-7910-9218-6 (hardcover)
   1. Saudi Arabia—Kings and rulers—Biography—Juvenile literature.
   2. Kings, queens, rulers, etc.   [1. Saudi Arabia—Kings and rulers.
   2. Saudi Arabia—History.]   I. Title.  II. Series.
   DS204.25.R44 2006
   953.805092′2—dc22              2006010613

Chelsea House books are available at special discounts when purchased in bulk quantities for businesses, associations, institutions, or sales promotions. Please call our Special Sales Department in New York at (212) 967-8800 or (800) 322-8755.

You can find Chelsea House on the World Wide Web at http://www.chelseahouse.com

Text design by Erik Lindstrom
Cover design by Takeshi Takahashi

Printed in the United States of America

Bang FOF 10 9 8 7 6 5 4 3 2 1

This book is printed on acid-free paper.

All links and Web addresses were checked and verified to be correct at the time of publication. Because of the dynamic nature of the Web, some addresses and links may have changed since publication and may no longer be valid.

# TABLE OF CONTENTS

ARTHUR M. SCHLESINGER, JR.

# On Leadership

L eadership, it may be said, is really what makes the world go round. Love no doubt smoothes the passage; but love is a private transaction between consenting adults. Leadership is a public transaction with history. The idea of leadership affirms the capacity of individuals to move, inspire, and mobilize masses of people so that they act together in pursuit of an end. Sometimes leadership serves good purposes, sometimes bad; but whether the end is benign or evil, great leaders are those men and women who leave their personal stamp on history.

Now, the very concept of leadership implies the proposition that individuals can make a difference. This proposition has never been universally accepted. From classical times to the present day, eminent thinkers have regarded individuals as no more than the agents and pawns of larger forces, whether the gods and goddesses of the ancient world or, in the modern era, race, class, nation, the dialectic, the will of the people, the spirit of the times, history itself. Against such forces, the individual dwindles into insignificance.

So contends the thesis of historical determinism. Tolstoy's great novel *War and Peace* offers a famous statement of the case. Why, Tolstoy asked, did millions of men in the Napoleonic Wars, denying their human feelings and their common sense, move back and forth across Europe slaughtering their fellows? "The war," Tolstoy answered, "was bound to happen simply because it was bound to happen." All prior history determined it. As for leaders, they, Tolstoy said, "are but the labels that serve to give a name to an end and, like labels, they have the least possible connection with the event." The greater the leader, "the more conspicuous the inevitability and the predestination of every act he commits." The leader, said Tolstoy, is "the slave of history."

Determinism takes many forms. Marxism is the determinism of class. Nazism the determinism of race. But the idea of men and women as the slaves of history runs athwart the deepest human instincts. Rigid determinism abolishes the idea of human freedom—the assumption of free choice that underlies every move we make, every word we speak, every thought we think. It abolishes the idea of human responsibility, since it is manifestly unfair to reward or punish people for actions that are by definition beyond their control. No one can live consistently by any deterministic creed. The Marxist states prove this themselves by their extreme susceptibility to the cult of leadership.

More than that, history refutes the idea that individuals make no difference. In December 1931, a British politician crossing Fifth Avenue in New York City between 76th and 77th streets around 10:30 P.M. looked in the wrong direction and was knocked down by an automobile—a moment, he later recalled, of a man aghast, a world aglare: "I do not understand why I was not broken like an eggshell or squashed like a gooseberry." Fourteen months later an American politician, sitting in an open car in Miami, Florida, was fired on by an assassin; the man beside him was hit. Those who believe that individuals make no difference to history might well ponder whether the next two decades would have been the same had Mario Constasino's car killed Winston Churchill in 1931 and Giuseppe Zangara's bullet killed Franklin Roosevelt in 1933. Suppose, in addition, that Lenin had died of typhus in Siberia in 1895 and that Hitler had been killed on the western front in 1916. What would the twentieth century have looked like now?

For better or for worse, individuals do make a difference. "The notion that a people can run itself and its affairs anonymously," wrote the philosopher William James, "is now well known to be the silliest of absurdities. Mankind does nothing save through initiatives on the part of inventors, great or small, and imitation by the rest of us—these are the sole factors in human progress. Individuals of genius show the way, and set the patterns, which common people then adopt and follow."

Leadership, James suggests, means leadership in thought as well as in action. In the long run, leaders in thought may well make the greater difference to the world. "The ideas of economists and political philosophers, both when they are right and when they are wrong," wrote John Maynard Keynes, "are more powerful than is commonly understood. Indeed the world is ruled by little else. Practical men, who believe themselves to be quite exempt from any intellectual influences, are usually the slaves of some defunct economist. . . . The power of vested interests is vastly exaggerated compared with the gradual encroachment of ideas."

But, as Woodrow Wilson once said, "Those only are leaders of men, in the general eye, who lead in action. . . . It is at their hands that new thought gets its translation into the crude language of deeds." Leaders in thought often invent in solitude and obscurity, leaving to later generations the tasks of imitation. Leaders in action—the leaders portrayed in this series—have to be effective in their own time.

And they cannot be effective by themselves. They must act in response to the rhythms of their age. Their genius must be adapted, in a phrase from William James, "to the receptivities of the moment." Leaders are useless without followers. "There goes the mob," said the French politician, hearing a clamor in the streets. "I am their leader. I must follow them." Great leaders turn the inchoate emotions of the mob to purposes of their own. They seize on the opportunities of their time, the hopes, fears, frustrations, crises, potentialities. They succeed when events have prepared the way for them, when the community is awaiting to be aroused, when they can provide the clarifying and organizing ideas. Leadership completes the circuit between the individual and the mass and thereby alters history.

It may alter history for better or for worse. Leaders have been responsible for the most extravagant follies and most monstrous crimes that have beset suffering humanity. They have also been vital in such gains as humanity has made in individual freedom, religious and racial tolerance, social justice, and respect for human rights.

There is no sure way to tell in advance who is going to lead for good and who for evil. But a glance at the gallery of men and women in MODERN WORLD LEADERS suggests some useful tests.

One test is this: Do leaders lead by force or by persuasion? By command or by consent? Through most of history leadership was exercised by the divine right of authority. The duty of followers was to defer and to obey. "Theirs not to reason why/Theirs but to do and die." On occasion, as with the so-called enlightened despots of the eighteenth century in Europe, absolutist leadership was animated by humane purposes. More often, absolutism nourished the passion for domination, land, gold, and conquest and resulted in tyranny.

The great revolution of modern times has been the revolution of equality. "Perhaps no form of government," wrote the British historian James Bryce in his study of the United States, *The American Commonwealth*, "needs great leaders so much as democracy." The idea that all people should be equal in their legal condition has undermined the old structure of authority, hierarchy, and deference. The revolution of equality has had two contrary effects on the nature of leadership. For equality, as Alexis de Tocqueville pointed out in his great study *Democracy in America*, might mean equality in servitude as well as equality in freedom.

"I know of only two methods of establishing equality in the political world," Tocqueville wrote. "Rights must be given to every citizen, or none at all to anyone . . . save one, who is the master of all." There was no middle ground "between the sovereignty of all and the absolute power of one man." In his astonishing prediction of twentieth-century totalitarian dictatorship, Tocqueville explained how the revolution of equality could lead to the *Führerprinzip* and more terrible absolutism than the world had ever known.

But when rights are given to every citizen and the sovereignty of all is established, the problem of leadership takes a new form, becomes more exacting than ever before. It is easy to issue commands and enforce them by the rope and the stake, the concentration camp and the *gulag*. It is much harder to use argument and achievement to overcome opposition and win consent. The Founding Fathers of the United States understood the difficulty. They believed that history had given them the opportunity to decide, as Alexander Hamilton wrote in the first Federalist Paper, whether men are indeed capable of basing government on "reflection and choice, or whether they are forever destined to depend . . . on accident and force."

Government by reflection and choice called for a new style of leadership and a new quality of followership. It required leaders to be responsive to popular concerns, and it required followers to be active and informed participants in the process. Democracy does not eliminate emotion from politics; sometimes it fosters demagoguery; but it is confident that, as the greatest of democratic leaders put it, you cannot fool all of the people all of the time. It measures leadership by results and retires those who overreach or falter or fail.

It is true that in the long run despots are measured by results too. But they can postpone the day of judgment, sometimes indefinitely, and in the meantime they can do infinite harm. It is also true that democracy is no guarantee of virtue and intelligence in government, for the voice of the people is not necessarily the voice of God. But democracy, by assuring the right of opposition, offers built-in resistance to the evils inherent in absolutism. As the theologian Reinhold Niebuhr summed it up, "Man's capacity for justice makes democracy possible, but man's inclination to justice makes democracy necessary."

A second test for leadership is the end for which power is sought. When leaders have as their goal the supremacy of a master race or the promotion of totalitarian revolution or the acquisition and exploitation of colonies or the protection of greed and privilege or the preservation of personal power, it is likely that their leadership will do little to advance the cause of humanity. When their goal is the abolition of slavery, the liberation of women, the enlargement of opportunity for the poor and powerless, the extension of equal rights to racial minorities, the defense of the freedoms of expression and opposition, it is likely that their leadership will increase the sum of human liberty and welfare.

Leaders have done great harm to the world. They have also conferred great benefits. You will find both sorts in this series. Even "good" leaders must be regarded with a certain wariness. Leaders are not demigods; they put on their trousers one leg after another just like ordinary mortals. No leader is infallible, and every leader needs to be reminded of this at regular intervals. Irreverence irritates leaders but is their salvation. Unquestioning submission corrupts leaders and demeans followers. Making a cult of a leader is always a mistake. Fortunately hero worship generates its own antidote. "Every hero," said Emerson, "becomes a bore at last."

The single benefit the great leaders confer is to embolden the rest of us to live according to our own best selves, to be active, insistent, and resolute in affirming our own sense of things. For great leaders attest to the reality of human freedom against the supposed inevitabilities of history. And they attest to the wisdom and power that may lie within the most unlikely of us, which is why Abraham Lincoln remains the supreme example of great leadership. A great leader, said Emerson, exhibits new possibilities to all humanity. "We feed on genius. . . . Great men exist that there may be greater men."

Great leaders, in short, justify themselves by emancipating and empowering their followers. So humanity struggles to master its destiny, remembering with Alexis de Tocqueville: "It is true that around every man a fatal circle is traced beyond which he cannot pass; but within the wide verge of that circle he is powerful and free; as it is with man, so with communities." ●

# 1

# Humble Origins

**SAUDI ARABIA IS LOCATED IN THE MIDDLE EAST, NEAR IRAQ, IRAN, JORDAN,** and Egypt. It is home to the world's wealthiest family, the Al Sauds, after whom the country is named. But the country comes from humble beginnings. In fact, the Saudi royal family is descended from a line of poor farmers. And yet, in less than a century, this family has not only gained control of the country, but it has also gained massive amounts of wealth from a booming oil exportation industry. Wealth comes with a price; these riches are so new to the Saudi royal family that they often misspend their money instead of using it responsibly.

This wealthy new way of life clashes not only with the family's humble beginnings, but also with the Islamic way of life. The House of Saud follows a strict form of the religion of Islam—a religion that holds many rules and guidelines that must be followed in daily life. These rules come from Islam's holy book, the Koran, and everything in Saudi life is based on it. The Koran

Portraits of King Fahd and the Saudi kings who ruled before him look down on Saudi subjects waiting in National Guard headquarters in Riyadh, Saudi Arabia's capital city.

governs what students learn in school, how women are required to dress, and how people are required to behave.

For hundreds of years, the Koran's strict rules have been followed, and in the twenty-first century, Saudis are required to continue following these rules. But it is difficult to follow such an extremely conservative religion while possessing great riches. The Saudi royal family finds itself in constant conflict: They must follow the strict rules of Islam, yet their riches allow them to desire and have the lifestyles of the far more liberal Western world.

Even though Saudi Arabia has tried to isolate itself from the rest of the world, it is hard to keep the world out. The country's oil industry requires it to deal with Western countries such as the United States. As money flows into Saudi Arabia, some of the values and customs of the West trickle in with it. The Saudi royal family and other newly wealthy Saudi people find themselves torn between wanting a freer lifestyle and staying true to their Islamic faith.

Saudi Arabia was once a desolate area populated by nomadic herders. The Al Saud family has tried to stay true to their ancestry, an ancestry responsible for the formation of their country, but living in a modern world with unbelievable riches causes serious problems. The members of the royal family find themselves in a constant conflict between Islam and money. They also find themselves the targets of constant ridicule, as Western countries and Saudi Arabian citizens criticize how thoughtlessly they spend their money. However, a great deal of good has come out of the royal family's wealth as well. The healthy economy of Saudi Arabia has improved life for many of its citizens. More hospitals, schools, and modern buildings have been built, roads have been paved, and cities have become more modernized with better infrastructures. The Saudi military has become larger and stronger, which helps the country defend itself. Despite all the good that has come out of the royal family's incredible wealth, corruption still remains a large problem.

How did Saudi Arabia get to this point? How did one family get so much money and power? And will the royal family be able to hold on to all of this, or will it slip away? In order to understand the Al Saud family, Saudi Arabia, and its future, we must first look to the past, beginning with the origins of Islam.

## THE PROPHET MUHAMMAD

Faith—belief in Allah, the god of Islam—is the most important thing in a true Muslim's life. Nothing, not even money or power, compares to a Muslim's relationship with God. Islam dominates not just Saudi society, but the societies of most of the Middle East. Just like the royal family of Saudi Arabia, however, Islam's origin is humble and elusive.

The prophet Muhammad greatly influenced the development of the Islamic religion. Surprisingly, he derived some of what he taught from a Christian monk and Judaism. Near the end of the sixth century, a boy was born in Mecca, a huge trading city and caravan oasis that drew people from all over the Middle East, people of many different beliefs and ways of life. At this time, the people of Mecca worshipped many gods. They did not believe that there was just one god, as the prophets of the Old and New Testaments taught. The Christians and Jews of the time both believed in the Old Testament, which makes up the first half of the Christian Bible today.

When Muhammad was six years old, his parents died and he went to live with his uncle, who was a merchant. His new family expected Muhammad to learn from his uncle and become a merchant as well, working with him when he came of age.

Being a merchant did not mean simply setting up shop and selling products. Merchants traveled in caravans and sold their goods all over the peninsula of Arabia. This was a very dangerous job. Bedouins often raided the caravans, killing the merchants and stealing their goods. Bedouins were nomadic herders who saw the caravans as an easy source of food and other products they needed to live in their hostile environment. Raiding caravans was part of their way of life for hundreds of years. It was also an inevitable part of life for merchants. Muhammad probably learned about desert warfare while traveling the dangerous caravan routes.

Muhammad met a Christian monk named Bahira, who considered Muhammad gifted, despite his wild demeanor and lack of education. Bahira failed to convert Muhammad to Christianity, but the impact he made on Muhammad lasted a lifetime. He did convince Muhammad that there was only one god and taught him about the great prophets of the Old

Testament—prophets such as Abraham, Moses, and Solomon, who are still important to Muslims today.

Soon after Muhammad turned 40, he became deeply depressed. He could no longer bear the injustices he continually saw around him: poverty, homelessness, brutality, and inequality. Muhammad felt that these injustices were the price society paid for its pagan beliefs. He left the merchant trade and spent his days praying in a nearby cave. One day, during his prayers, he felt his chest constrict and found it difficult to breathe. As he struggled for breath, he made a guttural sound: *qur'an.* This is now the name of the central religious text of Islam—the Koran—and it means "to read or recite."

Muhammad had divine revelations for some time and believed the angel Gabriel sent messages to him from God. These messages revealed the word of God, which became the Koran, the holy book of Islam.

At first, Muhammad was unsure of his calling. Converting people who believed in many gods to a belief in one god was difficult. Most of Muhammad's family shunned him, although his wife supported him and believed he was truly a messenger of God. Despite numerous plots against his life by those who adhered to pagan beliefs, Muhammad refused to give up his faith. He expanded his message into lessons on brotherhood and the equality of man. He taught that slaves were equal to their masters and the lower class was equal to the upper class. This was welcome news to slaves, but many slave owners and members of the upper class didn't condone Muhammad's teachings.

Despite constant threats against his life, Muhammad accepted an invitation to the city of Medina to help bring peace to two warring tribes. His journey between Mecca and Medina in A.D. 622 has since become the most important journey in Islam. It is called the *Hegira* and literally means "flight." The Hegira marked the beginning of the Islamic calendar and perhaps the beginning of Islam itself.

More than 2 million Muslim pilgrims from around the world travel to Mecca on a pilgrimage called the *hajj*. Here, thousands perform evening prayers inside the Grand Mosque, Islam's holiest shrine.

Once in Medina, Muhammad calmed the rivalry between the two tribes. He also met with a group of people, Jews, who believed in one god. Through this interaction, Muhammad adopted many Jewish customs and traditions into his own religion. For example, he set aside a Sabbath or holy day. He taught Muslims to face Jerusalem when they prayed, and he insisted on three obligatory prayers. However, when the more educated Jews of the time ridiculed Muhammad for his lack of education and poor knowledge of the Old Testament, Muhammad broke his ties with the Jews. He changed the Sabbath day to Friday and urged all Muslims to face Mecca when praying. He also began a month of fasting, called *Ramadan*, and the *hajj*, the pilgrimage to Mecca.

He became known as a conqueror and reformer, but he is best known as a messenger of God on Earth. Muhammad died in A.D. 632, but today, the religion he founded is the most rapidly growing religion in the world.

## MUHAMMAD IBN ABD AL-WAHHAB AND THE BIRTH OF THE WAHHABI SECT

The religion of Islam founded by Muhammad became the sole religion of Arabia. Today it's the way of life, the very essence of Saudi society. However, Arabia was a divided country for a long time.

Just as Protestants and Catholics have fought for centuries in the name of Christ, the Sunnis and Shiites have fought for centuries in the name of Muhammad. Hostilities between the Sunnis and Shiites date from the years after Muhammad's death. Both believe in Islam, but the two groups followed different leaders. The majority followed the Umayyad dynasty and came to be known as Sunnis. The rest are known as the Shia faction, or the Shiites.

Tribes fought against each other in bloody, ruthless battles. They fought over land and religious beliefs. Even though they were all considered Muslim and practiced Islam, the Sunnis felt they were practicing the true Islam, and the Shiites felt that their own beliefs corresponded more closely to the truth.

In the mid-eighteenth century, a young scholar named Muhammad ibn Abd al-Wahhab became a *Hanbali*. A Hanbali adhered to the strictest of Sunni Muslim laws and opposed the more recent and often more liberal practices that had been encroaching on Islam. Some of these practices included loving saints and their tombs, trees, and wells. When people focused their prayers and respect on their saints and on objects rather than on God himself, it was considered idolatry. A Hanbali also saw extravagance in worship and luxurious living as extreme evils.

Muhammad ibn Abd al-Wahhab began teaching his new ideas in his hometown in the Najd (Nejd) area, where foreign traders had not yet brought in and established Western ideas. Most of the people were farmers who struggled to grow crops in this inhospitable land of hot and desolate desert and barren hills, with no access to the sea beyond. It seemed like a good place to start preaching his strict Muslim ideas, but even the people here felt that those ideas were too extreme. Just as happened to the Prophet Muhammad, Muhammad bin Abd al-Wahhab's own family drove him out. He took refuge in a nearby town called Diriyah, under the protection of Muhammad bin Saud, the emir of Diriyah, whose descendents would become the rulers of a greater country 200 years later. The emir ruled this small region and was highly respected. Today, an emir is the governor of a city or province.

The people of the Najd area, including the Saud family, grew dates and not much else. These fruits were the mainstay of their diet. They were constantly attacked by Bedouin raiders, just as the prophet Muhammad had been attacked by the Bedouins a thousand years earlier.

At this time, in the eighteenth century, Islam had splintered into many sects. Some areas didn't even believe in Islam. People worshipped objects, rather than any one god. They wore charms to keep away evil and practiced astrology. Muhammad ibn Abd al-Wahhab saw this all around him and felt it was his mission to teach true Islam, the way the Prophet Muhammad had done over a thousand years earlier. When al-Wahhab had lived a year with the Saud family, he and Muhammad bin Saud united to convert people to Islam. This alliance would later be referred to as the Wahhabi Reformation of Islam; Wahhabism is practiced by the Saudi royal family today.

Together they visited nearby Arab tribes and villages, determined to convert as many people as they could. Not only did they wish to convert people back to the true Islam, but also they wished to unite the tribes and people under one god and eventually unite the entire Arabian Peninsula. The two men were a strong force. Muhammad ibn Abd al-Wahhab was the spiritual leader and spokesperson and Muhammad bin Saud was the military leader and protector of the sect. Their beliefs and ideologies soon became known as the Wahhabi Doctrine, named after Muhammad ibn Abd al-Wahhab. The current Al Saud dynasty and the country named Saudi Arabia derive their names from Muhammad bin Saud.

The two men managed to spread their rule and the Wahhabi Doctrine over most of northern Arabia. They even captured the holy city of Mecca and the city of Medina. While there, al-Wahhab and bin Saud destroyed many tombs and shrines that were associated with the Muslim hajj, or pilgrimage. They felt that people were worshiping the actual shrines and not worshiping the one true god.

The Wahhabi Doctrine spread to the Persian Gulf region, into the areas now known as Oman, Kuwait, and Qatar, and even to India, but the sect could not seem to win over the Rashid family and the western part of the Arabian Peninsula. Al Saud, al-Wahhab, and their followers were confined to the central and eastern portions of Arabia.

The Rashid family had the backing of the powerful Ottoman Empire in Turkey. The Ottoman Empire was spreading, working its way into the Arabian Peninsula. It, too, was a Muslim empire, but its people did not believe in the Wahhabi Doctrine. Together, the Rashid family and the Ottoman Empire were a strong force, and it seemed that the Wahhabi Doctrine would not survive.

Battles between tribes and even within the Al Saud family went on for years. In 1875, after much conflict and bloodshed over who would rule the city of Riyadh, the youngest son of King Faisal became king. His name was Abd al-Rahman (or Abdul Rahman) bin Faisal Al Saud. There were constant battles with the Rashid family for control of the city of Riyadh.

King Abdul Aziz Ibn Saud is pictured in 1922, during the Desert War. The king's defeat of the rival Rashid family was the genesis of the nation of Saudi Arabia.

Finally the Al Saud family was sent into exile; they lost control of the city and any hope they had of unification. Little did they know that Al Saud's and al-Wahhab's vision would succeed, through the efforts of the son of Abdul Rahman bin Faisal.

In 1902, his son, Abd al-Aziz (or Abdul Aziz) bin Abd al-Rahman Al Saud, later known as Ibn Saud, captured the capital city of Riyadh in a bloody battle, and the Rashid family began to crumble. This was the birth of Saudi Arabia as we know it today.

# 2

# Desert Kingdom

**TODAY, MANY PEOPLE THINK OF SAUDI ARABIA AS A RICH AND MODERN** country, and in many ways it is. The major cities in Saudi Arabia have beautiful, modern buildings complete with air-conditioning, a recently added luxury. In other areas of the cities are adobe buildings reminiscent of earlier times.

Until 1945, Saudi Arabia was considered poor and "back-ward." Called the homeland of Islam, it is where the prophet Muhammad was born and where the holy city of Mecca is located. Other than that, Saudi Arabia was seen as a desert with very little to offer. In fact, it wasn't even called Saudi Arabia until 1932, when the ruler Abdul Aziz ibn Saud renamed the country after his family. Before that, it was sim-ply called Arabia.

When Abdul Aziz ibn Saud battled against other tribes to unite the country, he did not have the wealth and status of the present-day king. In time, however, things would change. As his vision became reality, wild Arabia would be united under one god and under one ruler.

Today, Saudi Arabia supplies much of the world with oil, or "black gold." This newfound wealth has changed the lives of many Saudis, but most of the power and wealth go to the ruling government, the House of Saud. The Saudi royal family has made many positive changes for its country and the people. Among the dangers of wealth, however, are corruption and hypocrisy, and the Saudi royal family has been criticized for these very faults.

## A NEW TIME

> Who will ride at my side on this perilous venture?
> Who will risk life and limb to expel Al Rashid?
> Sixty answered my call, young and brave, one and all.
> With all of our strength, we will give what you need;
> We will stand by your side when the battle is joined
> Until each of us falls—or Riyadh is freed.

This is a small section taken from a lengthy poem written in honor of King Abdul Aziz, who, after capturing Riyadh in 1902, boldly proclaimed that he was the new emir not just of the small Riyadh region, but of the entire peninsula of Arabia. In the eyes of this new emir and his followers, they succeeded only because God wanted them to succeed. The Saudis are proud of their history, a history that can still be easily recollected by many elderly subjects. The bloody battle this poem details made a young man a king and founded the kingdom of Saudi Arabia.

Abdul Aziz ibn Saud was born in Riyadh in 1880. When he was 10 years old, the Rashid family drove his family out. The family fled to a refuge near Rub' al-Khali (the Empty Quarter) in the eastern part of the Arabian Peninsula. It is said that young Abdul Aziz and his sister were hidden away in saddlebags carried by a camel. The family lived among a poor tribe called the Bani Murrah. Abdul Aziz learned to ride camels and horses and

Today, oil is the major economic tie between Saudi Arabia and the United States. Pictured above, an ARAMCO official watches progress at a rig at the al-Howta oil field.

to shoot rifles. He also observed and learned how to deal with other tribal Arabs, something that would prove invaluable later in his life.

The family was eventually given asylum by the sheikh of Kuwait and moved to a fishing port near the head of the Persian Gulf. Here, Abdul Aziz learned about the Ottoman Empire and those who controlled the Arabian Peninsula— the Rashid family. By the twentieth century, the Ottoman Empire, backed by British rule, was creeping into many Arab countries. The Arabian Peninsula was one of the last places it did not control. Some of the Arab sheikhs made treaties with the British, but young Abdul Aziz did not want to be protected by foreign Christians, nor did he want dependency on the Ottomans, whom the Wahhabis saw as untrue Muslims.

Abdul Aziz had bigger ideas and a grander plan for his country. He wanted to retake Riyadh from the Rashid family and realize the dream his great-grandfathers and father had envisioned. He wanted to unite the peninsula of Arabia and make the Wahhabi Doctrine and Sunni Muslim law the chosen doctrine and law of the Islamic religion and Arabia. He wanted to regain the land of his forefathers despite all obstacles. Calling this a jihad, or holy war, Abdul Aziz resolved to unify the ranks of his nation under the banner "There is no God but Allah and Muhammad is the Messenger of Allah."

## THE TAKING OF RIYADH

It is said that in 1902, riding camels, Abdul Aziz and a band of 60 followers raced to his ancestral capital and took it over. Abdul Aziz was just 22 years old. The story itself is frequently told and is perhaps the most dramatic of all modern stories told about Saudi Arabia.

Under cover of night, Abdul Aziz and his cousin, Abdullah bin Jelawi, and several other volunteers stealthily approached a part of the city wall that they knew they could easily scale unobserved. The wall was adjacent to the house of a man who had served Abdul Rahman, Abdul Aziz's father, some years before, when the Saud family had still ruled in Riyadh. The man and his wife helped Abdul Aziz and his men get to the Rashid palace across the city's rooftops.

Abdul Aziz was looking for one member of the Rashid family in particular—Ajlan Rashid, the emir. Armed with rifles, Abdul Aziz entered Ajlan Rashid's harem. The women and slaves were terrified and quickly told Abdul Aziz the location of Ajlan's bedroom. Abdul Aziz stormed the bedroom of his enemy and found Ajlan's wife and sister. When the wife of Ajlan realized that the son of Abdul Rahman had come to reclaim his birthright, she told Abdul Aziz how many guards were in the palace and described her husband's morning routine. Some people wonder why this woman so readily betrayed her husband. She was probably more afraid for her own safety than her husband's. Rather than killing the women, Abdul Aziz locked them in a cellar and waited until morning to attack Ajlan and capture the city.

At dawn, after prayers, Ajlan emerged from the mosque into the street. When Ajlan was in the open, Abdul Aziz gave a loud battle cry and rushed from the palace to attack. Ajlan fled, with Abdul Aziz and his companions in hot pursuit. Abdul Aziz quickly cornered Ajlan, who defended himself until the sword of Abdullah bin Jelawi killed him.

The unexpected attack and the death of their leader demoralized the Rashid army, whose leaders assumed that such an assault could only have been mounted by a large and well-equipped force. Thinking that the residents of the city had welcomed the return of the Al Saud family, the army surrendered.

When Abdul Aziz took control of Riyadh on January 15, 1902, he burned 1,200 people to death and spiked the heads of other political and tribal enemies as a lesson to the people.

Although Abdul Aziz won that bloody battle, it took him 30 more years to truly unite the Arabian Peninsula. This process involved many more horrific battles, including Bedouin raids and wars between the Saudi-Wahhabi and other contenders for power.

At the turn of the twentieth century, Arabia had so many rulers that they could not all be documented. Abdul Aziz and his loyal followers had to defeat these tribal leaders one by one. First they defeated the Ottoman-backed Rashid family. In 1906, they gradually won control over the tribes of central and eastern Arabia. Abdul Aziz conquered the kingdom of Hijaz (or Hejaz) and took control of the holy cities of Mecca and Medina between 1924 and 1926.

Soon, Abdul Aziz became the most respected leader in Arabia, though some of this may have been more out of fear than true respect. Abdul Aziz personally executed 18 rebellious tribal chiefs. He chose his provincial governors for their brutality, not their compassion. To tighten their grip on the kingdom, these governors executed 40,000 people and amputated the limbs of another 350,000 out of a population of 4 million.

## KEEPING CONTROL

With so many warring tribes, it seems hard to fathom how one man and a small group of supporters took over a country and retained their power. Now that he was the king of Arabia and leader of the Wahhabi sect, Abdul Aziz first saw to it that Wahhabi Islam was strictly enforced and followed. His followers included many who seemed to enjoy fighting and winning. Abdul Aziz used religious beliefs to reinforce their desire to protect their new king and all he stood for.

Many saw Abdul Aziz as brave and strong, having conquered so much in a short time. His courageous exploits and personal magnetism drew people to him; thousands of Arabs loved and obeyed him. It was believed that if he had won so victoriously, Allah himself must have blessed him.

> On that night long ago, when the time came to act,
> I knew in my heart what it was to be free;
> The greatest good fortune in life for a man is
> To know he has reached for the best he can be.
> Whatever might follow that cold, moonless night
> We would know we had fought for a cause that was right.
>
> —*excerpt from the poem celebrating*
> *Abdul Aziz's taking of Riyadh*

Abdul Aziz was skilled not just in the martial arts such as hand-to-hand combat, but also in the "marital arts." He married and divorced so many women, it's hard to keep track of all of them. To Westerners this seems like a most peculiar practice, but during Abdul Aziz's day, marriage was used to seal peace and retain unity among the tribes he had defeated. The law of the

King Abdul Aziz, pictured in 1934, is known as King bin Saud in the West. The words *bin* and *ibn*, often used interchangeably, mean "son of."

Koran, however, states that a man may have only four wives at once, so after making peace, Abdul Aziz divorced his new wife and returned her to her home with gifts.

Abdul Aziz had nearly 300 wives during his lifetime. Many of these women he married for only a day. He probably never saw their faces, as women were required to remain veiled even on their wedding night. Despite the brief contact, it was said that every woman who married Abdul Aziz fell madly in love with him and loved him for the rest of her life. This is part of the legend of Abdul Aziz ibn Saud and how he conquered Arabia.

Always thinking of ways to unite the tribes under one king, Abdul Aziz created a religious organization called Ikhwan, which meant "brotherhood." Members of the Ikhwan were persuaded to give up their Bedouin way of life, which meant giving up camel nomadism and settling in one place. By doing so, they were obeying Wahhabi teachings. They never actually became farmers, but they did settle in small agricultural villages where Abdul Aziz had more control over them and could call upon them to serve him. Without the Ikhwan, the Saudis probably couldn't have united Arabia in such a short time. Ironically, the Ikhwan would eventually become unruly and bloodthirsty and turn on Abdul Aziz.

After capturing Asir, the kingdom between Hijaz and Yemen, Abdul Aziz was unable to conquer the rest of the Arabian Peninsula. On September 22, 1932, he declared that Arabia was now Saudi Arabia and that he was its only king. He attempted to capture Yemen in a brief war a couple of years later, but this proved futile. Abdul Aziz knew his limits; he seemed satisfied that the dream of his forefathers had now become reality.

King Abdul Aziz ibn Saud was not a rich man, even though he was king. The new Saudi Arabia was still a poor country. Abdul Aziz united the country through his devotion to Islam, but his puritanical beliefs could not withstand the wealth and Westernization that his beloved country would soon face.

CHAPTER

# 3

# King Abdul Aziz—A New Kingdom

**JUST AS THE SANDS IN A DESERT SHIFT AND CHANGE, SO DID THE LEADERSHIP** of the Arabian Peninsula. What was once wild territory governed by numerous nomadic tribes suddenly became a united country with one name, one king, and one government. Saudi Arabia was born; the country and its king, Abdul Aziz ibn Saud, governed by strict Islamic law.

In 1912, King Abdul Aziz had attempted to organize young men from the different tribes into an army to work for the common good of not just the people but also the new country. This was a daunting task because it required bringing together people who had been fighting each other for years. The new army consisted mostly of Bedouin tribesmen who only knew and understood desert combat; Abdul Aziz found it difficult to keep them under control. They killed, plundered, and raped, all in the name of Allah. In just a few years, they became so fanatical that even their own Bedouin Code of Law meant nothing to them. Sadly, Abdul Aziz saw his army, his warriors for Allah, become the very thing he and those of the Wahhabi sect despised—relentless renegades.

Abdul Aziz had other problems, as well. He'd killed Ajlan Rashid, but the Rashid family remained. The Rashid family had its own army in the north. Battles between the two families continued for ten more years. In the meantime, war on a much larger scale was being waged: World War I. The European armies cared little about the desert land of Arabia, but the British did want to enlist the cooperation of the new Arab leader in their fight against the Ottomans, who were still supporting the Rashid family. Two British men, Sir Percy Cox and William Shakespeare (not to be confused with the writer) befriended Abdul Aziz. The British often encouraged Abdul Aziz to attack the Rashid family's ancestral home in Hail. The British supported him in the war against the Ottoman Empire and the Rashid family, but they supported another man as ruler of the unified Arabian Peninsula. The British favored Husayn, the Hashemite sharif of Mecca, not Abdul Aziz. Obviously this did not please Abdul Aziz, who refrained from attacking Husayn only because the British opposed it, and Abdul Aziz had an alliance with the British.

Meanwhile, the Ikhwan were gaining more strength and power. They promoted their religious beliefs of Wahhabism and calmed the occasional rebellion, but they disobeyed Abdul Aziz's commands and broke the very laws of the religion they were trying to spread.

In 1919, the British turned their backs on Abdul Aziz and threw their support behind Sharif Husayn of Mecca, naming him the ruler of Arabia. The sharif of Mecca had already declared himself king of Arabia in 1917.

When a dispute arose over control of land between Hijaz and Najd in 1919, the sharif organized thousands of men and

King Faisal I of Iraq *(foreground)* is pictured at the 1919 Paris Peace Conference with *(from left)* General Nuri Es-Sa'id, Anglo-Irish soldier and Arabist Thomas Edward Lawrence and Captain Pisani of the French Mission. Lawrence was also known as T.E. Shaw and, more famously, as Lawrence of Arabia.

marched to the area. They easily overran a town called Turabah and thought they were victorious. Little did they know that the ruthlessness of the Ikhwan, under the leadership of Abdul Aziz, would change all this, and quickly. On the night of March 25, 1919, the Ikhwan attacked without warning. They recaptured Turabah and in the process killed 6,000 men. It is said that Abdul Aziz cried openly at the sight. Abdul Aziz ordered the Ikhwan not to pursue Husayn's fleeing army to the town of Taif. Surprisingly, they obeyed.

In 1920, Abdul Aziz turned his attention to the Rashid family. In this, he once again demonstrated his strong character and his faithfulness to his religion.

An 18-year-old boy was the ruler of the Rashid family. He became the head of the household only after a number of murders occurred, including the murders of his father and cousin. He was weak, both physically and in spirit, and just as afraid of his own family as he was of Abdul Aziz. Knowing how other family members felt about him, the young Rashid decided that his chances were better with Abdul Aziz than with his own family. As Abdul Aziz's army approached, he fled the city of Hail dressed as a woman and begged Abdul Aziz for mercy. Would Abdul Aziz show compassion or would he have the young boy beheaded? After all, this boy represented Abdul Aziz's archenemy, the Rashid family. Abdul Aziz showed great mercy and restraint. He did storm the palace of Rashid, and a battle raged for several days. The Rashid family finally surrendered. Abdul Aziz could easily have had them all killed. Instead, he told them that if they surrendered, they would be pardoned.

In front of the Rashid family, witnessed by the Ikhwan and many others, Abdul Aziz said something amazing: "I wish to assure you that you are as my sons and that you will live in Riyadh just as I and my sons live, no more, no less. Your clothes, food and horses will be like mine, if not better. There will be nothing in my palace or in the country that, if you want it, you cannot have. If any one of you has any doubt about what I say, let him speak."

No one said a word. After a few more words of promise, Abdul Aziz extended his hand to the Rashid family. He won his enemies over with his kindness. Sticking to his promises, Abdul Aziz fed the people of Hail and took the widow of the former Rashid ruler as his own wife. He also adopted all of the widows and children, a thousand in all! The intense rivalry between the House of Rashid and the House of Saud was over.

Now Abdul Aziz had to deal with his own creation, the Ikhwan. No longer obeying Abdul Aziz, they attacked villages, cities, and innocent people all over northern Arabia. Many people were so terrified of the Ikhwan that the people of a town would pack and leave if they heard of the Ikhwan's approach. Success after success only encouraged their belief that they were God's warriors, eliminating all that was evil in the eyes of God.

Spoiling for a fight, Ikhwan raiders attacked a Wahhabi caravan—their own people. They killed the men, boys, and male babies and left the women wandering hopelessly among the corpses. Abdul Aziz had heard and seen enough. He brought together an army of loyal Bedouins and met the Ikhwan at the oasis of Sibilla on March 29, 1929. The battle itself was brief; the Ikhwan were outnumbered.

Although clearly defeated, the Ikhwan army did not go away. They reorganized and grew in number over the next year. But so did Abdul Aziz's army. Determined to put an end to the Ikhwan, Abdul Aziz mechanized his army. An Englishman named Philby, the import agent for Ford motor cars in Arabia, encouraged Abdul Aziz to use cars instead of camels. The sight of fast-moving metal machines in battle totally demoralized the Ikhwan. The old ways of Arabia were giving way to those of the West, to more modern times. How could a camel compete with a car? It couldn't and neither could the Ikhwan.

The Ikhwan leader, al-Duwaish, and his family sought refuge in Kuwait, where he surrendered with the condition that the British would take responsibility for all his women and children. The British agreed, and a man named Dickson took in al-Duwaish's family. Dickson then pleaded with Abdul Aziz to spare al-Duwaish's life. Abdul Aziz said he would spare al-Duwaish's life if all of the Ikhwan leaders were handed over to him.

When Dickson asked about al-Duwaish's family, Abdul Aziz responded, "His daughters will be my daughters, his sisters, my sisters." Again, Abdul Aziz took in the family of

# In 1936 and 1939, Abdul Aziz granted oil concessions to American companies, allowing them to explore and drill for oil.

his enemy, demonstrating to his country his compassion and devotion to Islam.

## UNITED SAUDI ARABIA

Although Abdul Aziz united the peninsula of Arabia, the last 20 years of his life would prove to be his loneliest and most desolate. The 1930s were particularly hard for the new king. The country had no money and the only income came from the taxes that pilgrims paid when traveling to Mecca from all over the peninsula for the yearly hajj. This was not enough to sustain a kingdom and its people. Some money also came in from oil, but the development of oil had only just begun.

The greatest need was food, in this country that could barely grow food. Saudi Arabia had to import food from other countries. Because Saudi Arabia had little money, the purchase of food left the country in debt to other countries. The situation seemed hopeless. Modern times and realities were plaguing Abdul Aziz, and he became more depressed.

Abdul Aziz was a great ruler, but he had no administrative experience. Now that he had united his country under Islam and one god, he did not really know how to operate it. His instinct told him to rule as he did in the desert. If a person asked him for money to help buy food or medicine, Abdul Aziz gave it to him. It never occurred to the great king to set up some kind of ministry to take care of the medical, social, and economic needs of many people.

The kingdom itself was isolated. The capital of Riyadh, in the middle of the peninsula, enticed few Westerners—in fact,

Five sons of King Abdul Aziz ibn Saud board a plane at Herne Airport in Hampshire, England, on August 31, 1945. From left to right are the Saudi ambassador to London, the future King Faisal, Amir Mohammed, the future King Fahd, Amir Abdullah Al Faisal and Amir Nawaf.

non-Muslims were not allowed into the city. Abdul Aziz himself had been out of the country just once, to visit Iraq.

In 1936 and 1939, Abdul Aziz granted oil concessions to American companies, allowing them to explore and drill for oil. The oil deposits of Arabia proved to be among the richest in the world, and Abdul Aziz used some of the income derived from them on national improvements. The greater part of his oil revenues, however, went to the royal family.

In 1939, World War II created more problems for the king. He decided the best stand for Saudi Arabia would be to stay

neutral. Cutbacks in oil production ensued because of the war
and America's focus on the war effort. Fewer people made the
pilgrimage to Mecca. The income from taxes subsided and the
kingdom was near financial ruin. When World War II ended,
the United States showed a renewed interest in Saudi oil. With
the help of the United States, oil production boomed and a cor-
dial relationship developed between Abdul Aziz and President
Franklin D. Roosevelt.

At this time, there was great concern for the Jewish and
Palestinian people. World War II had displaced millions of
Jewish people, and the battle over the creation of Israel grew
between Jews and Arabs. Abdul Aziz told Roosevelt he sympa-
thized with the Jews, but he felt they should have their Jewish
state in Germany, not Palestine. Roosevelt asked Abdul Aziz to
meet with the Jewish leader Chaim Weizman, but Abdul Aziz
refused, saying he was not the spokesperson for the Arab world.

Oil production increased dramatically during the postwar
industrial boom. From 1947 on, Saudi Arabia never had to worry
about debt, bankruptcy, or reliance on other countries—at
least, this is what was thought. History has proven otherwise.
Regardless, the money made from oil was more than anything
ever dreamed of by the king or his family. Rather than making
Abdul Aziz happy, though, this new wealth and his own children
broke his heart and made him a lonely, bitter man in the last
years of his life.

Each family member was given an allowance in the thousands of dollars, and soon the West became that much closer—
just an airplane ride away. The young Saudi princes, who had led
relatively sheltered lives in the desert until this time, discovered
grand cities such as London, Paris, and New York. With money
came luxuries: homes, cars, Western clothing, and women. With
money, the ideals of Islam that Abdul Aziz treasured seemed to
be forgotten.

When Prince Mousaad was caught dancing naked in a
fountain in Paris, he was immediately sent home, and Abdul

Moments after the death of King Abdul Aziz *(seated)*, his sons and grandsons spoke the words, "We pledge loyalty to you on the Book of God and the traditions of his Messenger" to the newly crowned King Saud *(right)*.

Aziz confined his son to the palace. Mousaad became angry with his father. Although unable to act upon his anger, it showed years later.

Another son, Prince Mishari, killed the British consul in Jeddah because the consul refused to give him some whiskey. As is dictated by Islam law, Abdul Aziz offered the family of the consul his own son's life. They refused, but Abdul Aziz felt his son should be punished and put him in prison. Mishari's brother, Saud, who became king after the death of Abdul Aziz, later pardoned the prince.

In early November of 1953, news spread that King Abdul Aziz was dying. His sons and grandsons left their homes all over the world and rushed to the king's bedside. On November 9, Abdul Aziz ibn Saud died surrounded by 40 sons and 60 grandsons. Just minutes after Abdul Aziz died, his eldest living son, Saud IV, was declared the new king.

The body of King Abdul Aziz was buried in the desert sand at Miqbarat al-Oud. Only two rocks marked his grave, one at his head and the other at his feet, because Wahhabi tradition stipulates that there be no inscription on the grave. He was buried next to his favorite sister, Nura—the sister he had shared a saddlebag with 60 years earlier, when they were exiled to Kuwait. He left behind him a dynasty of many princes and princesses, 6,000 family members, and a country filled with black gold.

Today there are no graves. The rocks have been covered by sand, and the king has returned to his desert once again.

# 4

# King Saud, the Black Sheikh: 1953–1964

**WHEN KING ABDUL AZIZ DIED, HIS SON SAUD INHERITED THE KINGDOM.** Scholars are not certain why Abdul Aziz chose Saud. Born in 1902, he was the second son, always living in the shadow of his older brother, Turki. Saud's mother, Wadha bint Hazami, was a member of the Bani Khalid tribe.

Abdul Aziz provided for the education of all his sons. At the time, this was called a court education, which simply meant that they were taught to read in Arabic. Part of this education included memorizing the Koran, which Saud did before his fourteenth birthday. Boys learned to read, write, and do arithmetic, but they also took lessons in desert warfare.

Turki was clearly Abdul Aziz's favorite son, not just because he was the oldest boy, but because he had become an expert horseman and a courageous warrior by the time he was 12 years old. Saud was often ill, and although he grew tall like his father, he was weak and had poor eyesight. Had Turki lived, there is little doubt that he would have been named king of Saudi Arabia after his father's death.

Just after World War I, the Spanish flu swept through parts of the Arabian Peninsula. The Al Saud family was hit hard. The flu took the lives of two younger sons and eventually one of Abdul Aziz's wives, who was the mother of Khalid, another son destined to be king. It also took the life of Turki. Abdul Aziz turned to Saud to take over the role of his older brother. Saud was not the horseman his brother had been, though he did join his father in battle against the House of Rashid and proved to be a brave fighter. In 1926, he rode again into battle with his father against the sharif of Mecca. During this battle, some say, four assassins surrounded Abdul Aziz and Saud and knocked Abdul Aziz unconscious. Saud protected his father and defended himself against the assassins, killing one and holding off the others until help arrived. Saud proved himself loyal to his father and family, but his reputation would change drastically over time.

Again, however, Saud faced competition with the younger Faisal. The term "sibling rivalry" can be applied to its fullest extent when it comes to the Saudi royal family. Islamic law states that a man can have as many as four wives. The sons all had the same father, but they didn't have the same mother, which made them half brothers. Perhaps sibling loyalty was not as strong as it might have been had the sons of Abdul Aziz had the same mother.

As king, Abdul Aziz had to assess each son's ability and utilize that son's strengths. Feelings were no doubt hurt when one son was chosen over another, which is exactly what happened between Saud and Faisal. Abdul Aziz chose Faisal to lead an attack on Jeddah. There was a foreign diplomatic community in Jeddah, and Abdul Aziz felt Faisal could best handle this particular situation because of his experience with foreign

In 1946, Faisal and his son Muhammad bin Faisal bin Abd al-Aziz Al Saud attended a Palestine conference in London, England. Faisal and his half brother Saud were rivals for their father's attention. While the king kept Saud in Riyadh as viceroy of Najd, Faisal traveled to Europe and the United States, gaining experience in foreign affairs and diplomacy.

governments. Saud felt slighted by his father and wrote to him of his anger. It was obvious to Abdul Aziz that he would have to divide the responsibilities up. He gave Faisal and his third eldest son, Muhammad, responsibility for the Ikhwan. He kept Saud in Riyadh and made him viceroy of the Najd. Although governing the area as viceroy was an important responsibility, Saud felt that his father did not favor him.

Saud's duties included upholding the Wahhabi code of behavior. Saud tried to emulate his father in his compassion toward the people and in handling disputes between tribes, but he lacked two important qualities: charm and intelligence. He may have been book-smart, but Saud lacked skill in the fine art of foreign policy and diplomacy, something in which Faisal was gaining experience. Perhaps Saud's lack of knowledge had more to do with the fact that Abdul Aziz himself never ventured from the Arabian Peninsula. His only contact with foreign diplomats came when they traveled to him. Much of what Saud knew, he learned by watching his father. Faisal, on the other hand, traveled to Europe and the United States. He understood Western ways and became fluent in English. These would become important things for a future king of modern-day Saudi Arabia to know.

Because of Saud's lack of knowledge in foreign diplomacy, he felt he was treated in a belittling way by some of the greatest leaders in the world. One of his first visits to Harry S. Truman, the president of the United States in 1947, proved to be a fiasco—at least, in the eyes of Saud. Although Saud wanted to discuss important issues concerning Palestine and other matters, Truman seemed more interested in what Saud was wearing, his mannerisms, and his entourage.

Much of the West had stereotyped the Arab population as being more interested in trinkets and baubles than foreign policy. Truman presented Saud with a World War II medal for meritorious service to the Allied cause. This was ridiculous, since Saudi Arabia had entered the war just two months before it ended, and not one Saudi saw combat. One good thing came from Saud's visit to the United States: Saudi Arabia's first U.S. embassy was established in Riyadh in 1949.

When Saud became king of Saudi Arabia, the 40 sons and 60 grandsons who were present at the deathbed of Abdul Aziz welcomed Saud to his new position and swore loyalty to him. Faisal even kissed him on the shoulders and the bridge of his nose, a sign of affection and respect. Faisal was just as loyal to the new king as anyone else. King Saud kept Faisal as the viceroy of the Hijaz and as foreign minister.

As King Saud assumed his new role, it was obvious to some that he could not be the kind of king this new country needed in order to survive. The Middle East was undergoing harsh changes in the early 1950s. The Arab nations wanted to get away from British and French imperialism, seeing the presence of these foreign nations in the region as the source of many injustices. Some Arab nations felt they had been exploited solely for the benefit of these Western countries.

What really angered the Arab world was the creation of Israel. Many Middle Eastern countries felt Arab land was stolen from them for its creation. To people like King Abdul Aziz and King Saud, this represented a great betrayal by a country they had once trusted—Great Britain. This betrayal led those in the Arab countries to rethink what had happened to them in the past.

The biggest issue was oil. As Iran concluded that its resources were being stolen by Great Britain and the United States, others also began questioning their alliance with these two countries. The British government was keeping the price of oil low, which created an industrial and economic boom in the West, particularly in western Europe, but it also kept the nations of the Middle East in underdevelopment and poverty. King Saud, like his father, decided to support and promote Arab and Islamic unity.

In the early 1950s, in the early years of the Cold War, extremists rallied in the Middle East and disputes arose between Arab nations such as Egypt and Saudi Arabia. There was also the threat of invasion by the Soviet Union to the north. One thing Saudi Arabia had in its favor was that the United States opposed the Soviet Union as much as it did.

About this time, Saud found himself in financial trouble. He had been spending so much money building palaces and mansions that he nearly ran his country into debt. He turned to ARAMCO (the Arabian American Oil Company) for help. In turn, ARAMCO won Congressional approval for a "tax credit" bill. This bill provided King Saud with a massive subsidy, money that normally the U.S. Treasury would have received. Unbeknownst to them, the American taxpayers made up for Saud's losses through taxation.

It was rumored that, when Saud finished building a $50 million palace, he joked that he should send a thank-you card to the American people. Dwight D. Eisenhower, then president of the United States, remained quiet over this matter. He saw King Saud as a way "in," a way to gain the loyalty of other Arab nations through his own invention, the Eisenhower Doctrine.

The Eisenhower Doctrine was developed to suppress Soviet expansion. It provided military assistance to countries threatened by Communism. Eisenhower, who became president in 1953, needed an Arab spokesperson and Saud would be that spokesperson. The two men met and discussed the benefits to Saudi Arabia if Saud supported this doctrine. In the end, Saud walked away with American tanks, aircraft, arms, ammunition, and the services of military personnel in training the Saudi armed forces, as well as a loan for $250 million. Eisenhower agreed to put pressure on Israel to withdraw from Gaza if Saud would be the spokesperson for the doctrine.

On his return to Saudi Arabia, King Saud made stops in Morocco, Tunisia, Libya, and Egypt. In Egypt he met with hostility: Egypt's President Gamal Abdel Nasser disagreed with much of what Saud had to say about the Eisenhower Doctrine, which created further dissension between the two countries, who were already in dispute. (Years later, many believe, King Saud arranged for the assassination of President Nasser. Saud's reputation was already sinking, and this attempt on the life of Nasser did not improve the situation. The evidence against Saud was indisputable. Although King Saud said he would launch an investigation, it never happened—some would say it

King Saud, photographed with U.S. President Dwight Eisenhower *(left)* and Vice President Richard Nixon in Washington, D.C., in 1957, agreed to support the Eisenhower Doctrine in return for U.S. military equipment and a loan of $250 million.

was because he knew he would be found guilty of an attempt on President Nasser's life and be disgraced. As the sole ruler of Saudi Arabia, he was able to prevent any investigation into this plot.)

What had Saud done for his people? There were no plans for the future development of Saudi Arabia, no reforms. His spending escalated; he spent $150 million to build the Forbidden City, a private city that included four separate palaces, one for each wife. It also included 32 mansions for his concubines, 37 villas to house his sons, schools, a hospital, a museum, a zoo, and the largest air-conditioning plant in the world. Inside, the palaces were decorated with reproductions of

Louis XIV furniture, tables inlaid with gold and silver, crystal chandeliers and fixtures, and Persian carpets. This complex was just one of about 50 of Saud's projects. His flamboyant spending did not go unnoticed. Many Saudis disliked Saud and the royal family. After all, many of the members of the royal family who claimed to be devout Wahhabi Muslims were breaking the basic laws taught by Islam. Saud was also overly generous to others with his wealth. He had been seen tipping hotel workers the equivalent of hundreds of American dollars. Unfortunately for the royal family, his bad reputation didn't remain with just him but spread to the rest of the Saud household. The royal family gained a reputation for extravagance.

Meanwhile, his younger brother Faisal observed all these occurrences. In 1958, the senior Al Saud princes realized they would face devastating consequences if they did not do something about King Saud. They approached Saud and asked him for his abdication, or resignation, from the throne. Although Faisal saw Saud's behavior as destructive to the royal family, he didn't necessarily want Saud to step down. Instead he wanted his brother to stay on as king but be more of a figurehead than a true ruler. All power and control of the kingdom would be handed over to Faisal, who would ensure that his brother remained in his control. King Saud agreed, but the agreement did not last long. King Saud did not like being just the figurehead of the royal family. He worked to gain support among his few loyal followers.

In the meantime, Faisal was busy strengthening the Saudi economy and repairing the damage his brother had done. He borrowed half a billion riyals (Saudi currency) from a Saudi banker and assigned the financial genius Anwar Ali to head SAMA, the Saudi Arabian Monetary Agency. His efforts eventually brought the kingdom out of debt.

Faisal's other important objective was to unite the Arab world. He declared that Saudi Arabia would maintain a neutral stance in international affairs, including those regarding Israel.

This latter resolution would be more difficult to uphold than fixing the kingdom's economy had been.

By 1960, Faisal's health was beginning to deteriorate. When he traveled to Switzerland for treatment, King Saud stepped in and took over until Faisal's return. When Saud became ill in 1961 and left for treatment in Europe and the United States, Faisal took over the duties and responsibilities of head of state. During Saud's absence, Faisal replaced Saud's sons, who had positions in the government, with senior princes loyal to himself.

No one seemed to know who was really in charge, and there was much confusion in Riyadh. The friction between the two rulers divided both the royal family and the government into two camps: those loyal to Faisal and those loyal to Saud. The division was apparent to other countries in the Middle East, who saw it as a sign that the royal family was on the verge of disintegrating and that the kingdom was ripe for a revolution.

To the south of Saudi Arabia lies the country of Yemen. One of the people supporting the country in its war to remain independent from Saudi Arabia was the former Egyptian president, Nasser. Nasser was now president of the union of Egypt and Syria known as the United Arab Republic. Nasser was also backed by the Soviet Union. While Faisal was again out of the country, Egyptian jets bombed towns just over the Saudi border, and Saud was unable to cope.

At the royal family's urging, Faisal quickly returned and the situation began to change. The first reform Saudi Arabia ever saw was put into place. It was called the Ten Points of Policy and was enacted on November 6, 1962.

By the end of November, Faisal had broken all diplomatic relations with Egypt. The air raids increased. By 1963, Yemen was said to have 30,000 Egyptian troops at its disposal. King Saud and his supporters were still vying for a place in the government and it was still unclear who was the true king. Faisal had served as prime minister while Saud was king. Faisal stood his ground. He made stronger decisions, especially in the fight

In 1957, King Saud (photographed that year) founded Riyadh University, renamed King Saud University in 1982. The university has allowed women to enroll since the early 1960s.

against Yemen. Saud realized that he was losing any support he might have in the royal family. Saud's sons instigated conspiracies to overthrow Faisal. One attempted coup was thwarted.

Faisal, feeling tremendous pressure from his family and his country, left Riyadh on a journey overland, seeking solitude away from the confusion. During this time, more than 100 Al Saud princes met and discussed what should happen to their family and the government. They decided that Saud should abdicate his throne and Faisal should be the sole ruler. It seemed to them that Faisal had everyone's best interests at heart and was clearly working to make changes that would protect and benefit Saudi Arabia and the way of life of its citizens. Saud neither agreed to this nor abdicated the throne. Regardless, the Al Saud family recognized Faisal as the new king and placed Saud under house arrest. Still defiant, Saud tried to gather supporters. He failed and, with his wives and a number of sons, Saud was exiled to Athens, Greece. He died there in 1969.

Until recently, the royal family of Saudi Arabia never acknowledged Saud's role as king. His reputation in his later years for incompetence and extravagance overshadowed all the good he'd done in his earlier years. At one time, his portrait was not displayed anywhere in Saudi Arabia. All references to him or his reign were removed from books. The Saudis seemed to be embarrassed to talk about him and referred to him as "the black sheikh of the family."

Perhaps King Saud had trouble in handling the conflict created by living life as a devout Muslim on the one hand and having the riches of the world on the other. While he had the four wives allowed by Islamic doctrine, he also had up to 100 concubines, or mistresses. He spent most of the kingdom's money, about $200 million a year. Yet others have described him as being deeply religious, a good father to his people, and a staunch opponent of Communism. These opposing aspects of his personality and behavior show just how complex a man

King Saud really was, and they suggest the difficulty of ruling a country that was undergoing rapid and extensive changes.

Today King Saud is recognized among the kings of Saudi Arabia. His picture is now displayed in public places. His name is no longer deleted from books, and buildings are being named after him. King Saud's achievements include: protecting the country's independence and safeguarding its identity; establishing ministries in education, agriculture, commerce, and industry; paving the roads; developing the army; and founding Koran memorization schools.

# 5

# King Faisal, the Hero: 1964–1975

IF SAUD WAS KNOWN AS THE DISGRACE OF THE FAMILY, FAISAL WAS considered its hero. He was born in 1906. Abdul Aziz sent him to Europe just after World War I, which gave him a wider worldview than his brother Saud. What Saud didn't do for his country, Faisal did. He improved its economic, industrial, and agricultural condition by launching agricultural projects that included the Irrigation and Drainage Project and the Sands Project in Al Ahsa, in the kingdom's eastern region. This was combined with the Haradh Agricultural Project, the Abha Dam Project in the south, the Aforestation Project, the Animal Resources Project, and the Agricultural Credit Bank to improve conditions in the country. During King Faisal's reign, the area used for agricultural purposes increased greatly and the search for water sources was encouraged. The General Corporation

> I PRAY GOD TO GIVE ME
> STRENGTH AND MAKE ME
> WORTHY OF THE TRUST YOU PUT
> IN ME. . . . I AM ONE OF YOU,
> BOTH A BROTHER AND A SERVANT.
> . . . IN SERVING YOU, I PLEDGE
> YOU MY LOYALTY—I WILL BE JUST
> TO GREAT AND SMALL ALIKE.
>
> —King Faisal

for Petroleum and Minerals was established to help search for mineral deposits throughout the kingdom.

Faisal also improved conditions for women and increased their resources and higher education. Until this time, girls were not educated. Now girls were able to attend schools and young women had more opportunities to attend colleges and universities. He allowed the state to give financial aid and free textbooks to those who needed them. This did not go over well with some people, mainly extremist Wahhabis who believed girls should not be educated. Riots broke out preventing young girls from attending school. These riots, however, were minor compared to the riots that occurred at the introduction of television to the country.

The Koran forbids any representation of the human form. The portrayal of the human form on every television channel broke this law, or so many thought. Faisal argued that television could be used not for evil, but for good—it could help spread Islam.

In 1966, a riot broke out and young Prince Mousaad, the same prince who was earlier caught dancing naked in a fountain in Paris, was shot and killed by a policeman. Mousaad's father wanted the police officer killed, but after examining all the evidence, Faisal refused. He said the policeman was doing

Prince Faisal ibn Abd al-Aziz is shown on January 18, 1963, before becoming king. At the time, the prince was Saudi Arabia's Prime Minister and Minister for Foreign Affairs.

Israeli troops enter Gaza City in the Gaza Strip in June 1967. Like many Arabs, Faisal did not understand why the United States supported Israeli efforts to occupy what he considered to be Arab land.

his job and that Mousaad was part of the riot. The father of Mousaad said his son was simply standing by, perhaps in the wrong place at the wrong time. Faisal stood his ground on the issue. The anger and bitterness created by this decision would ultimately cost King Faisal his life.

Much of Faisal's success is credited to one of his wives, Iffat, who was the niece of one of Faisal's friends who had died. Faisal helped his friend's widow financially and soon the widow arrived in Riyadh at Faisal's doorstep, with Iffat and her half-brother, Kamal Adham. Faisal married Iffat just weeks later in an arranged marriage, as all marriages were arranged and still are in many instances today. Although it doesn't always happen, Faisal fell in love with his new bride. Many of his marriages to other women ended in divorce, but Faisal and Iffat were married for 40 years. Iffat was different from other Arab women because she was educated and Westernized. She encouraged her husband to send their sons to the United States for their education. Their daughters were also educated, even though there were no schools for girls in Saudi Arabia at the time. Their daughters memorized the Koran, learned to read and write in three different languages, and traveled throughout Europe. An old adage says "Behind every great man is a great woman," and many attribute Faisal's success to the influence of his intelligent wife. It was her influence that convinced Faisal to open schools for girls and allow the first women's organization, Al Nahda Women's Club.

Iffat's half-brother, Kamal Adham, was close to Faisal and one of the few men Faisal trusted. Kamal Adham advised Faisal on various policies and developed an impressive espionage system, one of the best in the world.

Faisal had a sometimes bumpy relationship with the United States, but he was flatly opposed to the Soviet Union. Faisal felt that both countries were invading Arab land. The United States supported the Jews in Israel rather than the Palestinians—land he saw as belonging to Arabs. The Soviet backing of Yemen and former Egyptian President Gamal Abdel Nasser was a continual threat. In 1967, though, Nasser and Faisal had a common enemy: Israel. During the Six-Day War, Israel occupied the Golan Heights, the Sinai, and Jerusalem. Of course, relations with the United States only got worse when President Richard Nixon told Faisal that he would pressure the Israeli government to withdraw from the territories they recently obtained if Faisal would convince Anwar Sadat, the president of Egypt, to reduce the Soviet military presence in Egypt. Faisal kept his word but Nixon did not. Israel refused to negotiate. This betrayal by America prompted Faisal to encourage an oil embargo against the United States.

Saudi men visit King Faisal's grave on the outskirts of Riyadh a few days after his assassination, in March 1975. Wahhabi tradition prohibits any inscription on the grave.

Hoping to develop stronger ties with other Arab nations such as Kuwait, Jordan, Bahrain, and the United Arab Emirates, Faisal scheduled a meeting with a group of Kuwaiti delegates on March 25, 1975, to discuss matters of unity and the oil embargo. A stranger entered as the men filed into the room. He was Faisal bin Musad, the brother of Mousaad, the young prince who had been killed by the policeman and whose death King Faisal wouldn't avenge. The king recognized the prince and bent his head down so the prince could kiss the bridge of his nose. Instead, the prince pulled a gun from his *thobe* (the long shirt worn by Arab men) and shot the king three times in the face. Faisal's reign came to an abrupt and sad end.

A quick trial found the brother of Mousaad guilty of murder and he was sentenced to death. He was beheaded with a golden sword, as was the right of Saudi princes.

Along with members of the Al Saud family, many influential people from all over the world attended his funeral, including Vice President Nelson Rockefeller from the United States. Many Saudis revered Faisal. He brought the country out of the past and into the present—a change that would continue into the reign of the next king, Khalid.

King Faisal accomplished many things during his rule, including increasing the amount of land for agriculture and expanding the search for sources of water, expanding higher education and providing more educational opportunities for girls, and safeguarding the country's independence and its identity.

# 6

# King Khalid, the Quiet One: 1975–1982

**EACH OF THE RULERS OF SAUDI ARABIA HAD THEIR OWN PERSONALITY AND** way of doing things. King Khalid was no different. Born in Riyadh in 1913, Khalid bin Abd al-Aziz was brought up under the watchful eye of his father, King Abdul Aziz Saud. This religious upbringing shaped his morals and his behavior and determined the way he ran the affairs of the country when he assumed power on March 25, 1975.

As soon as Faisal was assassinated, Khalid became king. When Khalid left Faisal's funeral, he cried openly in public and had to be supported by Anwar Sadat of Egypt and Yasir Arafat of the Palestine Liberation Organization (PLO). This open display of affection towards his brother reveals much about Khalid.

Little is known about how the Al Saud family chooses its king, but it is believed that maternal tribal ties play a part in the decision. A king was chosen from among the oldest sons of Abdul Aziz after much discussion and bargaining. If succession naturally fell to the next oldest, Khalid would not have been the rightful successor to the crown. Muhammad bin Abd al-Aziz was older than Khalid and should have been the rightful heir. Muhammad had a bad reputation and was referred to as Muhammad of the Twin Evils, as he was known as a drunk and a degenerate. The House of Saud was divided at this point. Muhammad's followers wanted him to become king, while Khalid's supporters felt Khalid was the best choice. Muhammad was offered the position of crown prince but turned it down.

In 1978, Muhammad shot his granddaughter to death and beheaded her boyfriend. His granddaughter had dishonored the family by being with her boyfriend, whom she loved. When they were caught they were arrested, and although the granddaughter and boyfriend hadn't broken any laws, Muhammad took the law into his own hands. This is often referred to as tribal law and not the law of Islam, which says people are allowed a trial. According to tribal law, the father, a grandfather, or other male relative has the right to deliver punishment for disobedience as he sees fit. Muhammad saw killing his granddaughter, a Saud princess, as his right. Although King Khalid and Prince Fahd tried to intervene on behalf of the princess, Muhammad was determined to see this through and bring honor to his family. Afterward, Khalid and Fahd acted as if nothing had happened and no one dared to bring charges against Muhammad. This caused much controversy in England, where a movie was made about the inhumane treatment of women, even those in the Saudi royal family.

It was probably best that Muhammad was bypassed in favor of Khalid as king. This was confirmed by Faisal himself, who had proclaimed Khalid his successor before he died. He defused two other potential threats in the House of Saud by naming his ambitious sons, Fahd, crown prince and deputy prime minister, and Abdullah, commander of the National Guard. Fahd later

King Khalid bin Abdul Aziz *(right)* is pictured on June 1, 1978, during talks in Geneva with Secretary of the Muslim World League Sheikh El Harkane *(left)* and Pierre Aubert of the Swiss Bunderstat.

became Saudi Arabia's king, and after his death, Abdullah took the throne.

Khalid was known as the quiet one, and many thought he would not make a good ruler, but he ruled with strength and persistence. He was consistent in his leadership and especially effective during the moments of crisis that arose during his rule. Unlike King Faisal, Khalid was more liberal in the way he governed. He gave more authority to his policy makers, most of whom had worked for King Faisal. He also allowed the governors more power and he informed the press of the rationale behind his policies. Before Khalid, kings didn't feel the need to explain why they passed a law or made a decision about the kingdom's policies.

Khalid kept the people of Saudi Arabia informed. He opened up the government to the people so that they would know some of what was going on in and with their country. Khalid saw important changes during his reign. The oil boom had started the year before, in 1974, and lasted until 1985. But even with tremendous amounts of money pouring in, he realized that the oil wouldn't last forever and turned his attention to other areas, especially agriculture.

One of Khalid's first accomplishments occurred in April 1975, when he settled debate over ownership of the land between Saudi Arabia, Oman, and Abu Dhabi known as the Al Buraymi Oasis. His reputation as a statesman grew, and people began to have more faith in the quiet king. King Khalid still faced many of the same problems Faisal had faced. He worked to keep relations between the Arab states strong and to keep the Soviet Union at bay. In 1976, Khalid visited the Persian Gulf states to promote unity and closer relations with Saudi Arabia's neighbors. These early visits probably helped in the creation of the GCC, the Gulf Cooperation Council.

Khalid suffered from many medical ailments. He had a heart problem and this may have hampered his ability to rule to his fullest extent. He relied on Fahd, who was already involved in foreign affairs and oil policy and had developed the League of Arab States, a peacekeeping force. Khalid had open-heart surgery in Cleveland, Ohio, and though it was successful, his health continued to deteriorate.

Developing the agriculture on the peninsula was one of Khalid's most significant domestic accomplishments. Until the late 1970s, although the Bedouin way of life was rapidly diminishing as more people settled near urban areas and worked for wages to make a living, agriculture was not fully developed. The Arabian Peninsula relied too much on imports of produce from other countries. Developing a strong agricultural base would provide not only food, but also jobs for the people of Saudi Arabia. Khalid wanted to modernize and commercialize agriculture. He spent money on the infrastructure, producing electricity and developing irrigation, drainage, and secondary

In 2000, members of the Gulf Cooperation Council (GCC) met in their annual summit and signed a defense pact to aid each other in the event of a military attack. The GCC is a product of King Khalid's efforts to maintain unity among Arab states.

road systems. He established places to market and distribute the produce. Land was given to individuals and to companies, who had to develop 25 percent of it in two to five years in order to win full ownership of the land. The Ministry of Agriculture and Water, the Saudi Arabian Agricultural Bank (SAAB), and the Grain Silos and Flour Mills Organization (GSFMO) aided in the development of agriculture. SAAB gave farmers interest-free loans, and the GSFMO purchased produce from the farmers.

King Khalid was not immune to crisis. In 1979, Egypt signed a peace treaty with Israel. Khalid, a strong supporter of Arab unity, was opposed to this arrangement and led economic sanctions against Egypt.

At this time, a group of 500 dissidents led by a Sunni named Juhaiman bin Muhammad bin Saif Al Utaiba seized the Grand Mosque in Riyahd and claimed the House of Saud had lost its legitimacy through corruption, ostentation, and imitation of the West. Khalid and the royal family were shocked by this take-over, as the Grand Mosque is considered sacred ground. Khalid and his advisors listened to the complaints of the dissidents and worked to resolve the problems throughout the peninsula that had led to the protest.

During his rule, Khalid established the King Faisal University in Dammam and Ummul Qura. He funded the building of grain silos and flour mills, and the kingdom's wheat production exceeded its consumption. He founded the Ministries of Industry and Electricity, built hospitals, and strengthened the army and National Guard.

## CHAPTER

# 7

# King Fahd, the Businessman: 1982–2005

**WHEN KHALID DIED IN 1982, THERE WAS NO DOUBT WHO WOULD SUCCEED** him on the Saudi throne. Fahd had already been a spokesman for Khalid and gained much exposure and experience. When he became king, he named Abdullah crown prince. The two sons who had always wanted to be rulers now had their turn.

King Fahd was the eldest son of Abdul Aziz and one of his favorite wives, Hussah al-Sudeiri. Abdul Aziz never divorced her, and she also had a lot of influence over the old monarch. She was involved in the upbringing of the sons she bore and taught them to be completely loyal to each other. She also met with her sons weekly to discuss current events and the royal family in general. Her seven sons were often referred to as the Sudeiri Seven. Their loyalty to each other has allowed them positions of power and control in the government. In order of age, they are: Prince Fahd,

# WITH THE BLESSING AND GRACE OF ALMIGHTY GOD AND WITH THE ASSISTANCE OF THE FAITHFUL SAUDI PEOPLE, WE SHALL CONTINUE THE WELFARE MARCH OF CONSTRUCTION AND DEVELOPMENT . . .

—King Fahd

Prince Sultan, Prince Abdul Rahman, Prince Naif, Prince Turki, Prince Salman, and Prince Ahmed.

King Fahd was born in the palace in Riyadh in 1923. Like the other sons, he received a court education. Unlike his half-brothers, Fahd was too young to join his father in the battles to unify Arabia; he had no military experience. His first government position was minister of education under King Faisal. This daunting job required not only the creation of an educational system in a country that had none, but incorporating girls into the educational system as well. He used the money from oil to build desperately needed schools around the country. Although many universities and schools were being built, the academic standards were very low. Fahd was interested in developing the higher education system and expanding the construction of universities, something he continued even after he became king.

In 1964, Fahd became the minister of the interior, a much more influential and politically powerful position than minister of education. This promotion was considered his next step toward the throne. He caught the attention of many people when a group of terrorists attacked oil installations in 1967. Fahd ordered the arrest of anyone suspected of being part of the attack and, when it was thought the terrorists had come from Yemen, he ordered thousands of Yemeni manual laborers deported on the grounds that their presence posed a threat to internal security. In another case in 1969, a group consisting mostly of army and air force officers planned a coup to oust

King Fahd is pictured in September 1990.

King Faisal. When their plan was uncovered, Fahd reportedly ordered that those involved be rounded up and executed.

Although Fahd effectively kept the peace in Saudi Arabia, Faisal was growing concerned about Fahd's suitability as the next king. Fahd had a gambling problem. At a hotel in Monte Carlo, many people witnessed the wealthy royal losing more money in one night than most people make in a lifetime. This arrogant and wasteful display damaged his chances of becoming the next king. King Faisal sent a message to Fahd, ordering his immediate return to Riyadh. Although Faisal threatened to disinherit him, Fahd continued gambling. Not only did his flamboyance upset his half-brother Faisal, but Fahd's behavior also broke the Islamic law that bans all gambling.

In the late 1970s, Fahd became the architect of Saudi foreign policy. He was torn between his pro-American leanings, his loyalty to other Arab nations, and his own family. Many Americans had been brought to Saudi Arabia to train the Saudi military, even though many Saudis, including some members of the royal family, resented their presence. Fahd, as spokesperson for the Saudi government, continually denied the presence of the American military in Saudi Arabia. The irony is that the Saudi government wanted American weapons and aircraft, but its armed forces didn't know how to use them. They could buy all the F-15s they wanted, but who would fly them? Certainly not young Bedouin camel herders. Without the American military training, the jets and weapons would be useless. Fahd knew that he needed the Americans but he also had to keep peace with his people, who were anti-American.

In 1980, the royal family attempted to distance itself from the United States. At this time, the United States was helping Afghanistan fight against the Soviet Union's occupation of that country. The Soviet Union was also backing the Palestinian people against Israel. The Saudi royal family questioned the United States' rationale for helping the Afghan people but not supporting the Palestinians. At the same time, Saudi Arabia accused the

Soviet Union of supporting one Islamic country and attacking another. The Saudi government could not have it both ways. The United States had been an ally to Israel in the past and would continue to be in the future. Fahd realized that he would always have to maintain a fine balance between his pro-American feelings and the feelings of those who were anti-American. If the United States were to one day completely support the Palestinian people, relations between Saudi Arabia and other Islamic nations would certainly change. However, the United States' loyalty to Israel would remain unchanged for many years to come.

In the late 1970s and 1980s, the royal family made decisions based on two issues: economic self-interest and the need to protect the kingdom from Soviet influence. Because of this, Saudi Arabia took a moderate stand on oil pricing. If it raised the price of oil, the United States and other countries felt the pressure and bought less, promoting inflation and affecting the economy. Because the royal family's assets were in dollars (not francs, marks, or gold) their profits were directly affected by any change in oil prices.

In recent years, after the United States launched the War on Terror, the price of oil has risen to record highs. Saudi Arabia is the world's largest oil exporter, so there are heightened concerns about keeping the oil facilities there safe and secure from terrorists. Because Islamic terrorist groups do not support the Saudi royal family's relationship with America, they want to destroy the oil exporting facilities that keep the relationship between these two countries strong. If these facilities are destroyed, it will affect the amount of oil Saudi Arabia can produce and export, and oil prices will be driven even higher.

## THE REIGN OF FAHD

When Fahd became king, the country had been in the middle of an oil boom that began around 1974, when Khalid was king. In 1982, the average export price per barrel of oil was above $30. The higher oil revenue meant more money for the royal family and thus development and construction in many areas increased. But because there was more oil being processed, a world oil surplus developed and the price per barrel dropped, resulting in a 20 percent drop in oil revenues. They continued to drop until the oil price crash of 1986.

Now Fahd had to deal with the repercussions. Saudi wealth decreased, and development around the country slowed down. Many of the developments started by Khalid during the boom became a burden. The high cost to maintain facilities and infrastructure could no longer be supported. The agricultural sector was hit hardest. Saudi Arabia had become self-sufficient in several major food grains, but the cost to do so was unjustified. Agricultural employment was on the decline and large conglomerates profited instead of the peasant farmers.

The reduction in Saudi wealth did not seem to affect Saudi Arabia's influence in the Arab world. Fahd himself became a major mediator in Arab conflicts. In 1989, Fahd helped in efforts to stop the fighting in Lebanon. He brought the entire Lebanese National Assembly, which included both Christian and Muslim deputies, to the Saudi resort city of Taif. The assembly couldn't meet in Lebanon because of outbreaks in violence between the military and politically motivated groups. Once at Taif, the assembly was able to negotiate and incorporate a new plan for reform and elect a new president.

The year 1987 brought important changes with Egypt. The Saudi government re-established ties with Egypt, and King Fahd visited that country in March 1989. The people of Cairo greeted him with enthusiasm, perhaps seeing a chance for peace and unity between the two Arab nations. Despite the fact that Egypt's ruler Nasser had once tried to overthrow King Faisal, Egypt was once again welcomed into the Arab community, with the welcome led by King Fahd himself.

King Fahd also reorganized the government of the Saudi kingdom. On January 3, 1992, he announced the establishment of four new systems: the Basic Government System, the

King Fahd walks with Egyptian President Hosni Mubarak *(left)* on March 27, 1989. The two were discussing a unified Arab position in preparation of Mubarak's upcoming meeting with U.S. President George H. W. Bush.

Consultative Council or Majlis Al-Shura Council System, the Provincial System, and the Council of Ministers System. Because of these new systems, the king and his ministers didn't have complete and total rule over the government or the country anymore. There were limitations that had never been implemented before, as well as some checks and balances. The state's legislative and executive authorities would be limited to specific terms, after which membership would be renewed or new members appointed for four-year terms.

The aim of the new systems was to tap the pool of qualified youths in the country. Fahd had noticed that much talent and intelligence was going unused in Saudi Arabia. Many young Saudi men and women were being educated outside of Saudi Arabia and their experience and knowledge could be a tremendous resource to the Saudi government.

The Basic Law of Government confirms that the system of government in the kingdom of Saudi Arabia is a monarchy. The Basic System establishes the general principles on which the kingdom of Saudi Arabia was founded. Article 1 clearly establishes the central tenets of the kingdom and has not swayed from the original beliefs laid down by Abdul Aziz when he first formed the united Saudi Arabia in 1932. Article 1 states: The Kingdom of Saudi Arabia is an Arab and Islamic Sovereign State; its religion is Islam and its constitution is the Holy Koran and the Prophet's Sunnah. Its language is Arabic and its capital is Riyadh.

The Basic Law gives power to the sons of the founder, King Abdul Aziz ibn Saud, and their offspring, and shall go to those who are most qualified. The king presides over the Council of Ministers, which controls the executive and organizational powers. Currently, the council is composed of 2 deputy premiers and 22 ministers. They run the affairs of state in the sovereignty, services, and development sectors. The sovereignty sector includes the Interior, Foreign, Defense, and Justice Ministries. The services sector includes the Ministries of Health, Education, Higher Education, Communications, Minister of Posts, Telegraphs, and Telegrams (PTT), Public Works and Housing, Labor and Social Affairs, Hajj, Islamic Affairs, Dawa and Endowments, Information, and Municipal and Rural Affairs. The development sector includes the Ministries of Finance, Commerce, Planning, Agriculture and Water, Industry and Electricity, and Petroleum and Mineral Resources. Linked to these ministries are several public agencies.

The kingdom has 13 regions controlled by local governors, all appointed by the king. Each governor acts in the same way as the governors of the states in the United States. Although it is similar in some areas to the kind of democracy we are used to in the United States, the Saudi government is quick to point out that the Saudi system of government, as defined under the Basic System and the establishment of the Consultative Council, is not a move towards Western-style democracy, much less an imitation of Western-style democratic reform. It is a development of the relationship between the leader and the people that is part of Islamic tradition.

The Consultative Council, or Majlis Al-Shura, formalized the people's participation in government in Saudi Arabia. The Majlis had already existed in the region for many centuries. Abdul Aziz and the kings after him all used this important aspect of Saudi governing. It allows the citizens of Saudi Arabia to air their grievances, complaints, needs, and suggestions to the king or a minister. The establishment of the council marked the first steps towards a more formal, broadly based involvement of the people in the kingdom's political processes. The Consultative Council consists of a speaker and 60 members selected by the king. In 2001, the number of members grew to 120. By 2005, that number was 150. Members of the council are also able to review legislation and domestic and foreign policies. In 2003, a royal decree was issued that gave these members the power to initiate legislation.

In 2004, King Fahd established a nongovernmental national human-rights advisory panel called the National Human Rights Association. Fahd formed the committee to help protect human rights because Islamic law is based upon the practice of protecting these rights. The panel of government-appointed committee members hears complaints about human-rights matters like torture and violence. This committee then works with the government to correct these issues.

The Saudi educational system also began a major cleanup. Many of the country's schoolbooks contained statements against Jews and Christians. The Saudis began removing the statements from classroom materials. Saudi Arabia began putting these measures into place to promote tolerance and further improve its image and relationship with the West.

In February of 2005, King Fahd once again made history when Saudi Arabia held its first local municipal elections. Although women were not allowed to run in the elections or to vote, and despite a turnout of only one-third of eligible voters, it was seen as a positive step. Saudi officials remain hopeful that not only will there be a bigger turnout in the future, but that someday soon women will be allowed to vote.

King Fahd's efforts to increase the pace of modernization while remaining firmly within the religious and cultural traditions of the kingdom continue even after his death.

## KING FAHD'S FOREIGN POLICY

One of the goals of King Fahd and his ministry was to bring about unity among the Arab countries of the Middle East. Just like his father and brothers before him, he realized the importance of uniting the countries of Islam. Separately, they are not strong; little good has come of their fighting with each other. The ultimate objective of King Fahd was a realistic peace. There must be compromise and negotiation and the end result should be fair to both sides. His position on the Palestinian and Israeli conflict reflected this view.

## THE PALESTINIAN-ISRAELI PROBLEM

After World War II and the vicious attack on Jews by Nazi Germany, millions of displaced Jews found themselves without a country, with no place to live or call home. They were sent to the land of Palestine, which is now Israel. Palestine was not an empty space waiting to be filled. It was the home of the Palestinian people. As the Jews were sent in, the Palestinian people were uprooted and displaced. The United States and Europe supported the Jewish occupation of Palestine, since it

In 1948, Arab refugees fled to Lebanon to escape the Arab-Israeli War being fought in the Galilee region in northern Israel, formerly a part of Palestine. The Arab population believes that the land was given to them by God through Abraham's son Ishmael. The Jewish population counters that God gave them the land through Abraham's son Isaac.

was also considered their homeland and seemed to be a reasonable place for the Jews to go. There were already Jews living in Palestine, but there were twice as many Arabs as Jews.

Many Arabs viewed this as racial cleansing. Palestinians were forced to leave their homes and businesses and were herded into small areas or kept at refugee camps. Both sides felt the land was theirs and called on the same story in the Old Testament, the story about Abraham, as evidence that God gave them the land. The Jews claimed the land was passed to them from Abraham through his son Isaac. The Palestinians claimed the land was passed to them through his other son, Ishmael. Both sides have attacked each other and both are guilty of terrorism and inhumane acts against each other.

What seems to confuse the Saudi kings is how the West can sympathize with one group of persecuted people, the Jews, and not show the same sympathy for another group of persecuted people, the Palestinians. If it was wrong for the Nazis to deny the rights of citizenship to the Jews, it must surely be wrong for Israel to deny the rights of citizenship to the Palestinians; if it was wrong for the Nazis to use the military power of the state to oppress a people, it must be wrong for the Israelis to oppress the Palestinians. If it was wrong for the Nazis to arrest Jews without due process of law, it must be wrong for the Israelis to carry out mass arrests of Palestinians without due legal process.

King Fahd had always supported Palestine, just as his father did. He planned to bring about peace in the region. In August 1981, Crown Prince Fahd created an eight-point peace plan. The points of the Fahd Plan were:

1. That Israel would withdraw from all Arab territory occupied in 1967, including Arab Jerusalem;
2. That Israeli settlements built on Arab land after 1967 would be dismantled, including those in Arab Jerusalem;
3. That freedom of worship would be guaranteed for all religions in the Holy Places;
4. That the Palestinian Arab people would have the right to return to their homes, and that those who did not wish to return would be compensated;

5.  That the West Bank and the Gaza Strip would have a transitional period, administered by the United Nations, for a period not exceeding a few months;
6.  That an independent Palestinian state would be established, with Jerusalemas its capital city;
7.  That all states in the region should be able to live in peace; and
8.  That the United Nations or member states of the United Nations would guarantee the carrying out of these provisions.

The Fahd Plan was significant in several ways. First, it showed that the kingdom of Saudi Arabia was prepared to take the initiative in trying to solve the problems posed by the creation of Israel. Second, it indicated the type of approach King Fahd would take to international diplomacy.

Many Arab nations did not like Fahd's plan because it gave the Jewish state a right to exist alongside a Palestinian state. Despite all the efforts of King Fahd and several other countries, including the United States, the conflict between the Jews and Arabs has continued and intensified. Extremists have used terrorism as their weapon of choice and carried out much of the violence, hurting and killing innocent people. There have been several attempts at peace between the rulers of both peoples, but the Israelis and Palestinians have seemed unable to reach any lasting agreements.

A great deal of the violence has occurred in the Gaza Strip, a territory of 146 square miles (360 sq. km) that lies on the Mediterranean coast, where Egypt and Israel meet. There were 21 Jewish settlements and 9,000 Jewish settlers located there; 1.4 million Palestinians live in Gaza as well. In 2004, Israeli Prime Minister Ariel Sharon announced a plan to remove all the Jewish settlements and Israeli troops in Gaza by the end of the following year. Sharon hoped that relocating the Israelis who lived in the Gaza Strip and turning the territory over to Palestinians would help the peace process proceed.

A year later, on August 17, 2005, Israeli troops began evacuating Jewish settlers who lived in Gaza. Many Israelis were defiant about leaving their homes, but all were eventually relocated. The Palestinian Authority president, Mahmoud Abbas, asked that Israel demolish most of the homes and buildings in the settlements left behind. The Palestinian people were overjoyed, and Israel seemed on the road toward creating Palestinian and Israeli states side by side.

But the Israeli pullout from Gaza did not automatically stop all of the violence. There were members of terrorist groups like Hamas and Islamic Jihad in Gaza who continued to launch attacks against Israelis. Clearly, there is still a long process ahead for Israel, the Palestinians, and their supporters if a peaceful coexistence is to be achieved. Saudi Arabia continues to support the Palestinian people.

## THE GULF WAR

Iraq declared victory over Iran after the Iraq-Iran War in 1988 but was economically hurt in the process. Hoping to regain stability through oil sales, Iraq's president, Saddam Hussein, became angry when Kuwait and the United Arab Emirates exceeded their OPEC quotas. Desperate to rebuild his economy, Hussein aggressively attacked Kuwait, first by demanding that all of Iraq's war debts be canceled, then by accusing Kuwait of stealing $2.4 billion worth of oil from an Iraqi oil field.

Because Saudi Arabia had backed Iraq against Iran, Iraq was sure that the Saudis would do the same in their efforts against Kuwait. When an attempt was made to resolve the problem, it became clear that Kuwait could not meet Saddam Hussein's demands. Saddam Hussein promised King Fahd that he would not invade Kuwait. When he went back on his word, it came as a shock to King Fahd. On August 2, 1990, Saddam

Hussein gained control of Kuwait. The United Nations condemned Iraq, and Saudi Arabia immediately sent troops to its borders. In Cairo, the Arab League also condemned Iraq. On August 12, Hussein announced that if Israel withdrew from Palestine, he would withdraw from Kuwait. Arab nations saw a similarity between what Iraq was doing in Kuwait and what Israel was doing in the former Palestine. This explains why Iraq later launched scud missiles against Israel.

Atrocities committed by Iraqi troops against the Kuwaiti people were relayed to King Fahd and the rest of the world. It became urgent that Saudi Arabia attempt to liberate Kuwait. In order to do this, Saudi Arabia would need the power and help of a bigger country—the United States. To ensure that the alliance was acting within United Nations authority, on November 29 the United States drafted a resolution declaring that if Iraq had not fully complied with earlier United Nations resolutions demanding its withdrawal from Kuwait by January 15, 1991, the alliance could use "all necessary means" to ensure compliance. This resolution (No. 678) was adopted by the United Nations.

In the middle of January, Operation Desert Storm began. Air assaults bombarded Iraq. In late January, Iraqi troops invaded a deserted town over the Saudi border but they were quickly repelled by Saudi troops. The alliance by Saudi Arabia, the United States, and other countries angered Hussein, and he retaliated by launching Scud missiles against Saudi Arabia. His main objective was the capital city of Riyadh, though most missiles never hit their intended targets. The war itself was over almost as quickly as it began. Although Iraq did much damage to Kuwait's oil fields, the alliance against Iraq nearly wiped out the country's army.

Many in the Arab world viewed King Fahd's reliance on the United States as dangerous. After the Gulf War, American troops were stationed in parts of Saudi Arabia and Bahrain, something that greatly upset anti-American Arab countries.

U.S. troops deploy across the Saudi desert on November 4, 1990, preparing to liberate Kuwait from Iraq in Operation Desert Storm.

But Saudi Arabia could not have expelled Iraq from Kuwait without the help of the United States and the alliance it formed with western European countries, England, and Canada. The relationship between Saudi Arabia and the West was firmly cemented.

# 8

# Saudi Arabia and the War on Terror

ON SEPTEMBER 11, 2001, THE WORLD WAS STUNNED WHEN TWO HIJACKED planes were flown into the World Trade Center towers in New York City. A third plane was crashed into the Pentagon building just outside Washington, D.C. A fourth plane, headed for an unknown destination, was also hijacked, but its passengers managed to stop the terrorists on board, and the plane crashed in a field in Pennsylvania. Thousands of innocent lives were lost, and American citizens, as well as people around the world, were devastated. It was the largest foreign attack on American soil since the Japanese bombed Pearl Harbor on December 7, 1941, which led to American involvement in World War II.

As the world reeled in shock at this gruesome act, King Fahd found his country once again in the spotlight. Suspicions were arising that Saudi Arabia had an involvement in producing, harboring, and funding terrorist acts of Islamic extremism. The world began to wonder: Was Saudi Arabia willing to fight against terrorism? Or was it involved in the problem itself? The pressure was on, and King Fahd faced new challenges.

## RELIGIOUS EXTREMISM AND SAUDI ARABIA

Some say that the threat of religious extremism is nonexistent in Saudi Arabia because the country already practices a stricter form of Islam than almost any other country in the world. However, one of the greatest threats to the House of Saud is that the family has no religious legitimacy as a ruling body. In Islam, hereditary power is forbidden. Some scholars of the Koran say that Islam calls for a democracy, complete with elections, not the current monarchial state held by the House of Saud. Although some changes are being made, and elections are being held, the royal family still holds a great deal of power and still controls much of what goes on in the country. Because the ruling family is so closely tied to Islam, many see this as an injustice to Islam. After all, the royal family has not always practiced what it preached.

As with the Bible, people interpret the Koran in different ways. These interpretations are seen as a threat to the royal family. Some claim that the Koran says things such as "consultation with the people in the affairs of state," while the royal family interprets these things differently, or perhaps ignores them altogether. The family's most dangerous enemies are the religious extremists who speak their minds and rebel against the system and the Saudi regime.

Today, religious extremists are found all over the world. Saudi Arabia has groups of extremists living inside and outside its borders. As investigations were made into the September 11 attacks, it was discovered that an Islamic terrorist group called Al Qaeda was responsible. It was also revealed that 15 of the 19 hijackers were Saudi nationals. These men had been under the direction of a terrorist leader named Osama bin Laden, who had been a Saudi national until his citizenship was revoked in 1995. His citizenship was taken away by the government after he claimed responsibility for terrorist attacks on U.S. bases in the cities of Riyadh and Dhahran. Terrorists also pose a threat to the Saudi royal family, who could be a possible target of terrorism in the future. Saudi Arabia has had to deal with many terrorist acts, some of them in the capital city of Riyadh, since September 11.

Since bin Laden was deprived of his citizenship, one of his main goals has been to overthrow the Saudi government—the government that he believes preaches the most conservative Islam in the world, yet is full of corruption, allies itself with the United States, and allows the U.S. military on its sacred land. The royal family fears bin Laden and his group of extremists, and this may explain its hesitation in acting more aggressively to stop them.

But even though Al Qaeda has declared its holy war on Saudi Arabia as well, with the royal family as a specific target, serious questions have been asked about whether the Saudis support terrorism. Many people suspect the Saudis of giving money to terrorist groups. Wealthy Saudis have given their money to individuals in need, or to charities they thought supported Islam and other causes. Some of the money instead has gone to terrorist groups and to schools teaching the hatred of Jews, Christians, and nonextremist Muslims. The Saudis are also thought to have supported a group of Islamic extremists called Hamas, which they do not view as terrorists but which the United States and other countries classify as terrorists, due to their violent actions.

Princess Haifa al-Faisal, the wife of Saudi ambassador Prince Bandar bin Sultan, was targeted in an investigation into the financial support of terrorists. Money that she gave to someone she claims she believed was sick and in need was traced to two of the September 11 hijackers. Her brother, Turki al-Faisal, who was a former chief of Saudi intelligence, appeared

Prince Bandar bin Sultan, former Saudi ambassador to the United States, attends the Red Sea summit in Egypt on June 3, 2003. Money given by his wife went to hijackers of the planes involved in the September 11 attacks on the United States.

on an American television show called *Connie Chung Tonight* to defend his sister. He explained that the princess thought she was only helping someone who needed money and that she didn't realize the money would instead go to support terrorists. It is still not known whether this story is true.

After rising speculations over wealthy Saudis supporting terrorist groups, King Fahd implemented some changes. He issued a royal decree in February 2004 that announced a new financial institution. This group would restructure how money was collected and distributed to charities. King Fahd banned money from being sent outside the country, and he also banned cash collections in public places such as mosques. He still believed in the Islamic law that Muslims should help each other financially, but he wanted to regulate how this help was distributed. Working with the United States, Saudi Arabia helped stop an organization called Al-Haramain, an Islamic foundation based in Saudi Arabia that collected money for terrorists. However, this group was able to spread into other countries and continue collecting money by disguising itself as a charity group. Clearly, there still remains a great deal of work to be done to stop funding terrorist groups.

Not all of the money raised by the Saudis goes to negative or questionable causes, however. On December 26, 2004, a huge earthquake that struck parts of Asia triggered a massive tsunami, giant and destructive waves. Many poor Asian countries were unprepared and thousands of people died. In early January 2005, the Saudis held a telethon that raised $77 million for tsunami aid and relief. Much of the money was donated by the royal family, including $5 million from King Fahd, $2.5 million from Crown Prince Abdullah, and $17 million from Prince Alwaleed bin Talal. The Islamic Development Bank also pledged $500 million toward tsunami aid, in addition to another $30 million pledged by the kingdom. Saudi Arabia agreed to work with the United Nations to coordinate how the aid money was gathered and distributed. Saudi Arabia was able to use its riches to help the tsunami victims and also to try and improve its image as a country that shares its wealth in positive ways.

### THE WAR ON TERROR

Speculations were made that Osama bin Laden had purposely chosen mostly Saudi terrorists to carry out the September 11 attacks on America. As the investigation into the attacks continued, it was believed that bin Laden was trying to make Saudi Arabia look responsible for the attacks, in order to weaken its relationship with the United States.

The United States gathered evidence that Osama bin Laden and members of Al Qaeda were hiding in Afghanistan. The ruling government of Afghanistan was the Taliban, a group of Islamic extremists who were sympathetic to Al Qaeda and allowed its members to train and reside in the country. The Taliban rose to power in 1992, after a period of civil war in Afghanistan. The Soviet Union's army had been occupying the country, and militant Afghan forces called the Mujahideen fended off the Soviets. But after the Soviets left, many different warlords began battling over control of Afghanistan. The Taliban were able to overthrow all of these warlords and take political power. They restored order to the chaotic country through the use of radical Islamic ideas. The group also reacted violently toward groups opposing it and its rule. By 1996, all opponents of the Taliban had been effectively overthrown, and the country was established as the Islamic Emirate of Afghanistan.

The Islamic Emirate of Afghanistan was recognized only by other Islamic countries like Pakistan, the United Arab Emirates, and Saudi Arabia. A great deal of support for the Taliban came from a major charity in Saudi Arabia. The amount is estimated at $2 million a year. The money from this charity was meant to fund humanitarian aid, like health clinics and support for orphans, as well as education—funds also went toward two universities. King Fahd even made a yearly gift to the Taliban of a large shipment of dates, one of Saudi Arabia's crops. It is clear that Saudi Arabia initially supported the Taliban and their rule in Afghanistan. After the September 11 attacks on the United States, Saudi Arabia declared that it no longer recognized the Taliban as the government of Afghanistan. The United Arab Emirates also made this decision.

Because the Taliban supported Al Qaeda, the United States decided to invade Afghanistan. In October of 2001, American troops began bombing Afghanistan and invaded the country, declaring a War on Terror. American forces were able to overthrow the Taliban, which allowed for a less extreme and more democratic government. During this time, Al Qaeda members worldwide continued issuing threats of more terrorist acts against the United States and other countries that it felt were against Islam. Since the start of the War on Terror, many Al Qaeda members and other terrorists have been captured or killed, and quite a few of them have been captured in Saudi Arabia by Saudi officials, but to this day bin Laden still remains free and in hiding.

As the United States continued investigating terrorism and Al Qaeda, it began to suspect Saudi Arabia's neighbor, Iraq, of secretly building weapons of mass destruction, such as chemical and biological weapons. The United States also wanted to liberate the Iraqi people from the tyrannical leadership of Saddam Hussein. On March 20, 2003, the United States invaded Iraq, and Saddam Hussein went into hiding. That December, Hussein was found in hiding and captured. Saudi Arabia allowed the United States to use its air space in the invasion of Iraq.

After the U.S. invasion, the Iraqi people elected a new democratic government, and it began drafting a constitution. Despite these advances toward bringing the Iraqis out of the shadow of their tyrannical leader, however, violence still grips much of Iraq. Insurgents who were angry at the invasion by

America and its allies began planting bombs and killing innocent people, sometimes even strapping the bombs to themselves
in suicide bombings. The insurgency still continues in Iraq as
Western troops struggle to get the situation under control.

As the War on Terror continues, Saudi Arabia finds itself
a target for not only terrorism but also intense international
scrutiny. Because they are an Islamic people who nevertheless
retain diplomatic relations with the United States, Saudis find
themselves targets of terrorism by other Islamic extremists.
There have been numerous terrorist bombings in Saudi Arabia
since the war started, most of them carried out by members of
Al Qaeda.

After the start of the war, several Western citizens, including Americans, working in Saudi Arabia and have been
captured and killed by terrorist groups. These groups have
demanded that Saudi officials negotiate with them, saying they
will spare the lives of their hostages if the Saudi government
in turn releases imprisoned terrorists. The Saudi government
has refused negotiations with these groups, and the hostages
have been killed, often by beheading. Americans are angry
that their own citizens, who were peacefully working in Saudi
Arabia, have been killed so brutally by these groups. The United
States has demanded that the Saudis try harder to stop terrorist
groups and to capture these extremist leaders. Saudi officials
have worked hard to aid their American allies and have success-
fully captured some members of terrorists groups. But many
Americans and people in other countries still believe that more
needs to be done by the Saudis to stop terrorism.

## THE SAUDI-BUSH CONNECTION

Much controversy surrounds the relationship between
the Saudi royal family and the Bush family. U.S. President
George W. Bush and his family consider the Saudi royal family "great friends" both personally and of all Americans. Of all
Arab nations why choose Saudi Arabia as close friends? Why

Osama bin Laden, whose Saudi citizenship was revoked in 1994, is the prime suspect in the September 11, 2001, terror attack on the United States.

would Saudi Arabia want to have a close relationship with a country that is the complete opposite of its conservative Islamic monarchy? The answer: oil.

George H. W. Bush, George W. Bush's father, was involved in the oil business before taking a job as CIA director under President Gerald Ford in 1976. At the same time, the Saudi royal family began investing in banks and real estate in Texas. The Saudi royal family was growing richer and richer as they sold more oil.

During the 1980s, when Ronald Reagan was president and George H.W. Bush was vice president, the United States helped the Saudis fund the Mujahideen, the militant Afghan group that fended off the Soviet Union's army, which was occupying Afghanistan. At the time, relations between the United States and the Soviet Union were still strained as a result of the Cold War. The United States wanted to see Afghanistan gain freedom from a country that was still under the Communist system of government—a system the United States strongly opposed. At the same time, Saudi charities that were used to fund Islamic groups were growing in number and strength. These charities funded many schools and programs that taught extremist Islam, which were programs that produced future terrorists like Osama Bin Laden.

The Saudi family in turn helped the Bush family. George W. Bush was a director of an oil company called Harken Energy in the 1980s. The company was doing poorly financially because the price of oil had dropped worldwide. The Saudi royal family and its investors provided the money necessary to keep the company afloat. At the time, in 1986, George H. W. Bush was still the vice president of the United States under Reagan, and he would later go on to serve one term as president.

Ties between the two families strengthened further when George H.W. Bush joined an investment and equity firm called the Carlyle Group. This group had a great deal of government contacts, which it used to get contracts, many in Saudi Arabia, that brought in a great deal of money. Both Bush men, as well as Bush and Reagan aides, worked with the company. The Saudis invested, and soon the company had received $1.4 billion from them. The Saudis also made contracts with a company called Halliburton Energy Services, which was run by Dick Cheney, secretary of defense under George H.W. Bush, and vice president under George W. Bush.

Saudi dollars have helped George W. Bush and many of his friends accumulate wealth. In exchange, Bush has offered help and protection to the Saudis. Shortly after the September 11 attacks on America, when air travel into and out of America was banned for several days, George W. Bush allowed a group of Saudis, including members of bin Laden's family (who were not known to be involved in terrorism), to be flown out of the United States, where they were staying at the time. None of these people were allowed to be interrogated or interviewed by American intelligence forces before they were secretly flown out of the country. Some of them, especially bin Laden's relatives, could have provided vital information to help find Osama bin Laden and determine if he had any other terrorist attacks planned. It was also believed that many wealthy Saudis were funding terrorist groups like Al Qaeda.

Many people criticize George W. Bush for putting his personal business interests ahead of the security and best interests of the country. Others believe that he does not want to alienate the Saudis and so he maintains a special relationship with them.

# 9

# King Abdullah

**KING FAHD ACTIVELY RULED SAUDI ARABIA UNTIL 1995. THEN HE SUFFERED** a serious stroke that left him impaired. He became noticeably frail and often seemed unaware of things that were going on around him. At this time, King Fahd became more of a figure-head of the Saudi monarchy. Because of his poor health, his half-brother and successor to the throne, Crown Prince Abdullah, became responsible for running much of the country.

## THE END OF KING FAHD'S RULE

King Fahd continued to attend meetings and receive some important visitors, but most of the duties and official trips fell on Crown Prince Abdullah. Fahd pledged that his country would help to strike down terrorists with an iron fist, especially since his own country had become a victim of bombings and other acts of terrorism. Fahd was able to travel on personal vacations and was sometimes away from Saudi Arabia for extended periods.

In May of 2005, Fahd fell ill and was hospitalized for symptoms similar to pneumonia. Although the king did recover, it was a sign that he was weak and unwell. He had already been hospitalized several times that year. Abdullah had been running the country, acting as monarch, and meeting with other world leaders. Quite a few of his meetings were with President Bush and other American leaders to discuss the future of oil production in Saudi Arabia and how to continue combating terrorism together.

Fahd's continual illnesses took their toll on his frail health, and on August 1, 2005, Fahd died. Reports were uncertain as to his exact age, but it was guessed he was between 82 and 84 years old. Leaders from all over the world came to pay their final respects to King Fahd, including Prince Charles of Britain, President Jacques Chirac of France, and President George W. Bush and Vice President Dick Cheney of the United States. President Bush referred to King Fahd as "my friend" and wished the new king, Abdullah, congratulations and success as he took the throne. President Bush and King Abdullah also promised that the close partnership between their countries, strengthened by King Fahd, would continue.

Thousands of mourners crowded around the mosque where King Fahd's body lay, paying their respects and chanting a special prayer for the dead. These people honored their dead king and his achievements, which included strengthening the economy, improving agriculture and education, cracking down on terrorism, and instituting municipal elections. His 23-year reign had brought much prosperity to Saudi Arabia, but it also led to controversy in the Arab world as many devout Muslims questioned whether a nation could remain true to Islam while also maintaining such strong ties with the radically different Western world.

King Fahd was buried wrapped in a brown robe in a cemetery in Al-Oud, where other members of the Al Saud family are buried, and was carried there by his sons on a wooden

Relatives of King Fahd perform special Muslim prayers at Riyadh's Turk bin Abdullah mosque in front of his shrouded body on August 2, 2005, the day following his death.

plank. As is the Islamic tradition, his burial place was marked with a small, plain stone that bears no inscription. Unlike the tradition in other countries where a leader dies, Saudi flags around the country were not lowered to half-staff. The Saudi flag carries the words "There is no God but Allah," and it is considered blasphemous to lower it. Saudi Arabia also followed the laws of Wahhabism and did not declare a national period of mourning. Many other countries, however, such as Egypt,

Iraq, Jordan, Pakistan, Kuwait, the United Arab Emirates, and Spain, where King Fahd liked to vacation, all declared some form of mourning period.

## KING ABDULLAH TAKES THE THRONE

When King Fahd died, his half-brother Abdullah was immediately named king. Defense Minister Prince Sultan was named crown prince. Abdullah was the son of Abdul Aziz and his eighth wife, Fahda bint Asi Al Shuraim. When he was young, he attended the Princes' School in the Royal Court. In 1963, he was the commander of the Saudi National Guard, and in 1982, he became the first deputy prime minister. In 1995, when King Fahd suffered a stroke, Abdullah became the de-facto ruler of Saudi Arabia. Abdullah is thought to be at least 80 years old, though, like Fahd, his exact age is unknown.

Because Abdullah had been acting on behalf of the ailing King Fahd for ten years, he was already accustomed to many of the duties of a Saudi king. He was officially enthroned on August 3, 2005. King Abdullah already had a great deal of experience regarding foreign relations. In 2002, he had suggested a plan called the Arab Peace Initiative, which he believed would help promote peace between Arab nations and Israel. His plan said that Israel should return the West Bank and the Gaza Strip to the Palestinian Authority, and in exchange there would be peace between Israel and the Arab states that were so violently opposed to it. Israel and a number of Arab nations protested the initiative. This plan was never put into action, but a few years after Abdullah's attempts, Israel did in fact return the Gaza Strip to the Palestinian Authority.

After becoming king, Abdullah also began to visit other Arab nations and Saudi Arabia's geographical neighbors, including Syria, Egypt, and Jordan. He knows that many other Islamic countries are wary of Saudi Arabia because of its close ties with the West. By traveling to these countries and talking with their leaders, King Abdullah hopes to improve relations with them. He wants to resume the quest for peace in the Middle East, and he feels the best way to achieve this is through the cooperation of all Arab nations. Clearly this will be a challenge that Abdullah will have to face for the rest of his reign as king.

One country Abdullah has visited often is America. Since 1976, Abdullah has been visiting America and meeting with presidents and vice presidents. Shortly after the death of King Fahd, Saudi Arabia pledged to continue the legacy of King Fahd by providing oil to the rest of the world at stable prices. President George W. Bush has named Abdullah a friend of his family and of America.

A few months after becoming king, Abdullah had his first interview on the American news program *20/20*. Barbara Walters, who is well known for her interviews of famous people, interviewed him. In the interview, King Abdullah expressed his strong disapproval for Al Qaeda, calling their activities "madness and evil." He pledged to the American people that he and his country would continue to hunt terrorists, and that they would not tolerate their activities. He also assured America that it had the continued support of the Saudis. His country, he claimed, had withdrawn support from organizations and institutions that supported extremism, including schools that taught hatred of nonextremist Islam.

King Abdullah also talked about the rights of women in Saudi Arabia and said that they were making progress. To illustrate his point, he stated that by conducting an interview with Barbara Walters, he was fulfilling a promise he had made several years earlier that he wanted to be interviewed by a woman when he became king. At the time of the interview, Saudi women still could not vote and needed permission to do other things, like travel or attend colleges and universities. They even needed permission to have surgery. King Abdullah promised that his country was actively moving toward reforms for its female citizens and said that it would take some time.

King Abdullah has fostered strong ties with the U.S. government, having visited top officials since 1976. Here, the Saudi foreign minister, Prince Saud bin Faisal bin Abd al-Aziz Al Saud (Prince Saud al-Faisal) meets with President George W. Bush at the White House on September 20, 2001.

He explained that Saudi Arabia was still very slowly allowing the world in and that people were still getting accustomed to many freedoms and customs that people in the West take for granted, like equal rights for women. He said that his country was still learning to balance the Islamic faith with modern advancements and democracy. Many Saudi citizens still did not trust America or its foreign policies, especially in regard to its support for Israel and the invasions of fellow Muslim countries Afghanistan and Iraq. He said that it would take time for Saudi Arabia to accept Western ways more readily, and also for relations among all nations in the Middle East to become peaceful.

As an example, he used the case of American democracy, pointing out that it took a long time to develop into the system we have today.

Barbara Walters then asked King Abdullah about Americans' concerns about the rising prices of crude oil. Prices had tripled over the past decade, and the Saudis were making a profit at the expense of countries that needed the oil. Abdullah offered assurances that measures would be taken to ensure fair pricing of oil.

It is obvious that King Abdullah was well prepared to take over leadership of his country as its monarch. But with his new position of power come many challenges. The continuing violence between Israel and the Palestinian people, the War on Terror in Afghanistan and Iraq, and strained relations between Saudi Arabia and other countries are all things King Abdullah must face while on the throne. Another key question: What will happen when Saudi Arabia runs out of oil? How will the Saudi royal family maintain its lavish lifestyle and stay in power when their main source of income disappears? Most important, how will Saudi Arabia maintain its relationship with America while still observing its traditional Islamic way of life? The future is never certain, and how the Saudi government and the royal family conduct themselves in foreign policy could help them or destroy them.

# 10

# Friend or Foe: The Future of Saudi Arabia

**SINCE THE TERRORIST ATTACKS ON THE UNITED STATES ON SEPTEMBER 11,** 2001, the world has changed in many ways, and one of the places that has changed a great deal is Saudi Arabia. The relationship between Saudi Arabia's royal family and the United States is continually being tested. Saudi Arabia, situated geographically in the midst of other Arab nations, finds itself torn between keeping Arab unity and taking a stronger stand with the West against terrorism.

The Saudis find themselves accused of supporting terrorism by some in the West, and yet these are the very people who most depend upon Saudi Arabia's oil for fuel. As the leader of Saudi Arabia, King Abdullah finds that he faces the challenges of keeping peaceful relations with his country's Arab neighbors while also catering to the desires of Western countries

# WHEN THE UNITED STATES BEGAN THE WAR ON TERROR IN AFGHANISTAN AND LATER INVADED IRAQ, SAUDI ARABIA FELT ITS LOYALTIES STRETCHED EVEN FURTHER.

like the United States—countries that support Saudi Arabia's oil-based economy.

The Gulf War proved that Saudi Arabia depends on the United States as an ally just as much as the United States depends on the continual supply of oil at low prices—if not more. And in the months following the attack of September 11 against the United States, in which 15 of the 19 terrorists involved were from Saudi Arabia, the royal family and its ministry have been scrambling to keep ties open with the United States. On October 4, 2001, Prince Sultan met with U.S. Defense Secretary Donald Rumsfeld and stressed that the friendly ties with the United States should remain intact. He denounced the actions of Osama bin Laden and Al Qaeda by saying "[b]in Laden has shown himself to be a terrorist and a criminal. Bin Laden is not a Saud citizen, and he does not represent the Kingdom of Saudi Arabia."

When the United States began the War on Terror in Afghanistan and later invaded Iraq, Saudi Arabia felt its loyalties stretched even further. How could the country maintain its relationships with other Islamic countries when it was pledging to support the United States in its attempts to eradicate Al Qaeda? The country was accused of and proven to have been supporting numerous Islamic extremist organizations, groups that more often than not bred terrorists who were intent on destroying the Western way of life through violent acts. The United States asked for help in fighting terrorism but isn't getting the kind of results from Saudi Arabia that it wants. Meanwhile, the prices of oil continue to climb, making fuel harder and harder to afford. Saudi Arabia hangs in a precarious balance with one of the countries most opposite to it in the world—the United States.

Then there is the question of Saudi oil reserves. Even though Saudi Arabia holds a quarter of the world's crude oil reserves, these supplies won't last forever. Scientists have estimated that these oil reserves will be sufficient for only the next 70 years or so. What will happen to the Saudi economy when oil wells start to run dry? The Saudi royal family relies on oil to keep their riches flowing in, and many of the princes and princesses seem to spend their wealth wastefully. The country must prepare for a possible economic crisis when oil reserves run low. If it does not continue to develop agriculture and other industries, Saudi Arabia as we know it today could disappear forever and just as quickly slip back into the impoverished country it once was.

The question of whether the Saudis continue to financially support terrorist groups troubles many people. It causes them to wonder whether the Saudis can be trusted to help in the War on Terror. Many of the world's Islamic extremist terrorists come from this country. How can the West trust Saudi Arabia to stop the spread of terrorism?

And while the country is taking steps toward democracy, like holding the first-ever municipal elections, it still has a long way to go. The country is ruled by a monarchy that upholds a very conservative form of the religion of Islam called Wahhabism. Women are still not allowed to vote in Saudi Arabia and still do not have other rights considered very basic to women in other parts of the world. Even though King Abdullah himself has said that reforms for women are coming, he has admitted that they will take some time to happen. There is limited freedom of expression. The royal family is the sole government of Saudi Arabia, and it monitors everything that is said about it and the country. If you were to ask a Saudi citizen his thoughts on the government there, he would probably respond positively and say that he likes it and the royal family. Even if he does not

A trader in the New York Mercantile Exchange oil futures pit shouts his order on June 20, 2005. Oil prices continued to rise.

believe this, this is what he will say, because if he answers negatively, he could be thrown in jail. Prisoners in Saudi jails are tortured, so the citizens of Saudi Arabia are careful not to risk imprisonment by complaining about their government.

It would seem that members of the royal family are not only afraid of losing their hold on the oil industry, but also on the people of their country. The senior princes don't allow political expression, particularly if it is negative. They developed SANG, the Saudi Arabia National Guard, whose sole purpose is to protect the royal family from a takeover. No one quite knows how many men are part of SANG, but it is estimated that the small army numbers between 50,000 and 100,000. Why would the royal family need so many bodyguards if it didn't feel threatened? Do they feel threatened by their relationship with the United States? Bin Laden was quoted as saying that the Saudi royal family was one of his targets, and that he was waging war against them. Is the Saudi family afraid that bin Laden and his fellow terrorists will make good on their word?

The fact that the Saudi family is able to maintain such a close and public relationship with the United States is in itself challenging. Like many Arab nations, Saudi Arabia's citizens generally have very anti-American feelings. The ways of the West, which are progressive, democratic, and constantly changing, challenge the traditional Islamic way of life, which is conservative and deeply devoted to its faith and to ancient tradition. Arab nations find it hard to coexist peacefully with nations like the United States, let alone allow the country's ways into their own homeland.

Arab countries are also strongly against Israel, which they feel unjustly took land away from Palestinians and destroyed the Palestinian state. The Americans, however, are strongly pro-Israel. It is well known that Saudi Arabia, like its Arab neighbors, sides with the Palestinian Authority. Other Arab nations can't understand how Saudi Arabia can trust and ally itself with the United States when the U.S. supports their enemy Israel. Will the fact that Israel returned the Gaza Strip to the Palestinian Authority begin to bridge the gap to peace between these two nations? If this peace happens, will it positively impact the relationship between Arab countries and the West? How will it affect the royal family's relationship with the United States? Will it make those ties stronger, or will the Saudis continue to insist that Israel should not be trusted?

Members of the royal family are not only torn in their loyalties to each other, the oil industry, and Islam; the country itself and its people are also torn. Because of the wealth created by the oil industry, there is now an educated middle class in Saudi Arabia. More young Saudis are being educated in the United States and experiencing firsthand the Western lifestyle—freedom of speech, the freedom to worship as they choose, and the freedom to disagree with the government, which are all things they cannot have in Saudi Arabia. In Saudi Arabia, this middle class is becoming increasingly discontented with the royal family. The royal family cannot control all the negative press about it, especially in other countries. Many Saudis are discovering unpleasant truths about the royal family, in particular its corruption and illegal activities. Many of them are also upset that the royal family continues to rule, even though Islamic law prohibits governance by a single family where positions are inherited.

Many Saudis are not willing to work, either, not when the money from the oil industry flows in so abundantly. They want a piece of this industry and, in some ways, feel they deserve it without having to work for it. The labor force in Saudi Arabia consists mostly of foreigners. They dig the ditches, pick up the trash, and drive the buses; all are jobs that many native Saudis feel are beneath them or simply won't do. Students at universities see themselves becoming businessmen and women. This means they'd like to become partners with companies outside the kingdom. The only way a foreigner can enter the kingdom is through an employer who sponsors him or her. Saudi Arabia does not allow tourist visas. These students see themselves becoming agents, getting the workers from overseas companies along with the profits.

Despite their lucrative ties with the United States, the royal family, especially the senior princes, tend to side with isolationism, especially when it comes to their people. They feel safer keeping the West at arm's length and isolating their citizens from outside influences. When foreigners are in the country, their living quarters are separate from Saudi citizens, and they cannot associate with Saudi nationals. The non-Western foreign workers often live and work on the job site and are exploited so badly that it is very hard for them to ever break their contract with a company. They are often forced to work until death.

As hard as Saudi Arabia tries to be modern, true modernity is a way of thinking, not a way to construct buildings or do business with other modern countries.

The royal family is constantly under attack. The senior princes, including the sons of Abdul Aziz ibn Saud, were raised in a time when Saudi Arabia was more isolated from the rest of the world. Their sons and grandsons are living in today's world. While preaching the Koran and Islamic law in one breath, some members of the royal family break laws, oppress their subjects, and act in opposition to their stated beliefs. Saudi citizens don't need Western newspapers and magazines to see this. It's happening in front of them, in their own country. Despite the royal family's tremendous wealth, poverty in Saudi Arabia is still evident. The royal family spends millions on luxurious palaces while some citizens are hungry and homeless.

Many students blame the royal family for the country's "backwardness." Students today will be tomorrow's businessmen and women, leaders with families of their own. The royal family seems ill-prepared to deal with the future dissidence that is inevitable.

Internal discontent, a war on terrorism, extremist religious leaders, dwindling oil supplies, Western ways and values, corruption, jealousy among family members, and a general uncer-

Saudi women leave a polling station after voting in elections in February 2006, where six women were running for places on the board of the Chamber of Commerce and Industry in al-Qatif. Just a year earlier, women were barred from voting.

tainty have plagued the House of Saud in recent times. Finding a balance between wealth and Islamic faith has been hard, if not impossible. The country is involved in a balancing act every day, finding itself teetering first in one direction, then the other. The scrutiny of the world has put a great deal of pressure on the Saudis. No one can predict exactly what will happen.

Saudi Arabia has seen incredible change and rapid growth in a short period of time. It remains an introverted society with a government system headed by aged members of the royal family. Saudi Arabia's relationship with the United States is a mutually beneficial business deal. It has so far survived despite Saudi Arabia's lack of democracy or accountability and its intense Islamic conservatism. But these relations have been tested by terrorism and by the fact that Saudi Arabia is believed to support the very terrorist groups it claims it is fighting against. The world's demand for oil increases, and every day the Saudi supplies are diminishing. The very survival of the Saudi regime is at stake on many different levels.

King Fahd led his kingdom through its most prosperous time until his death in the summer of 2005. After Fahd's death, King Abdullah found himself, in his 80s, as the monarch of Saudi Arabia and the head of the world's wealthiest family. He also found himself in the midst of controversy because of his progressive thinking about Israel. Even before officially becoming king, Abdullah believed that a peaceful agreement could be reached between Israel and the Palestinians and the rest of the Arab world. He surprised many in the Arab world in an interview with the German magazine *Der Spiegel*. He said, "For more than fifty years, no Arab had thought that it was possible to live together with Israel. Today we have arrived at the point where Arabs and Israelis can begin a new life together. We have a real chance for peace." Many Arabs do not agree with Abdullah's position. These statements, and moves towards reforms for women, could increase his unpopularity and harm Saudi Arabia's relations with other Arab nations. In addition, of course, there is the problem of what Saudi Arabia's main industries will be once the oil supplies run out. King Abdullah and his successors have their work cut out for them.

The ideas Abdul Aziz once had for his united Arabia seem to be long forgotten. The discovery of oil has changed the country forever, from its leaders down to its common citizens. Discontent and frustration hover over the House of Saud as it tries to make peace within its own confines, with its people, and with the countries of the world.

Despite its corruption and seemingly backward ways, the Saudi royal family has improved the overall well-being of its citizens by building schools and hospitals and incorporating some modern ways into Saudi society. As in any family, some members are more productive than others. Some have big hearts and grand ideas while others can't seem to do anything right. Like everyone on earth, members of the royal family are only human despite the vast riches they possess. No one in the royal family is invincible, and all of them have human imperfections.

No one can predict what will happen to Saudi Arabia in the future. The members of the House of Saud, the richest family in the world, must determine the kind of future they want to have, and they must work toward achieving it themselves.

# CHRONOLOGY

| | |
|---|---|
| **1871** | The Ottoman Empire takes control of the province of Hasa. |
| **1880** | Abdul Aziz ibn Saud is born in Riyadh. |
| **1891** | The Al Saud family is exiled to Kuwait by the Rashid family. |
| **1902** | Abdul Aziz Al Saud takes control of Riyadh, bringing the Al Saud family back into Saudi Arabia. |
| **1912** | Abdul Aziz Al Saud founds the Ikhwan (Brotherhood). |
| **1913** | Abdul Aziz Al Saud takes Hasa from the Ottoman Empire |
| **1921** | Abdul Aziz Al Saud takes the title Sultan of Najd. |
| **1924** | Mecca regained |
| **1925** | Medina retaken. |
| **1926** | Abdul Aziz is proclaimed King of the Hijaz in the Grand Mosque of Mecca. |
| **1928-30** | The Ikhwan turn against Abdul Aziz Al Saud but are defeated by Abdul Aziz Al Saud. |
| **1932** | The areas controlled by Abdul Aziz are unified under the name Kingdom of Saudi Arabia, and Abdul Aziz proclaims himself king. |
| **1933** | King Abdul Aziz's eldest son, Saud, is named crown prince. |
| **1938** | Oil is discovered and production begins under the U.S.-controlled ARAMCO (Arabian-American Oil Company). |
| **1953** | King Abdul Aziz Al Saud dies and is succeeded by the crown prince, Saud bin Abd al-Aziz Al Saud. The new king's brother Faisal is named crown prince. |
| **1960** | Saudi Arabia is a founding member of OPEC (Organization of Petroleum-Exporting Countries). |

| 1964 | King Saud is deposed. Crown Prince Faisal bin Abd al-Aziz Al Saud is named king. |
| 1975 | King Faisal is assassinated by his nephew Faisal bin Musaid bin Abd al-Aziz Al Saud; he is succeeded by his brother Khalid bin Abd al-Aziz Al Saud. |
| 1980 | Saudi Arabia takes full control of ARAMCO from the United States. |
| 1982 | King Khalid dies of a heart attack and is succeeded by his brother Crown Prince Fahd bin Abd al-Aziz Al Saud. |
| 1987 | Saudi Arabia resumes diplomatic relations with Egypt (severed since 1979). |
| 1993 | King Fahd decrees the division of Saudi Arabia into thirteen administrative divisions. |
| 1994 | Islamic dissident Osama bin Laden is stripped of his Saudi nationality |
| 1995 | King Fahd has a stroke; the daily operations of the country are entrusted to Crown Prince Abdullah bin Abd al-Aziz Al Saud. |
| 1999 | Twenty Saudi women attend the session of the Consultative Council, the first time women are allowed to do so. |
| 2001 | Saudi Family attempts to donate $10 million to relief efforts in New York City. Mayor Rudolph Giuliani does not accept the money. |
| 2002 | Money used by the terrorists in the September 11 attacks on the United States is traced back to Saudi princess Haifa al-Faisal. The Saudi royal family vehemently denies that it knew its money would be used to fund terrorism. |

**2003**   After declaring that Iraq has the capacity to make chemical and biological weapons of mass destruction, the United States invades Iraq. Saudi Arabia allows the United States to use its air space.

**2004**   Filmmaker Michael Moore releases a documentary, *Fahrenheit 9/11*, detailing the aftermath of the September 11 attacks. In the film, he exposes the relationships between the Bush family and the Saudi royal family, and how the Saudis are suspected of funding and supporting terrorism.

**2005**   *January.* Saudi Arabia holds a telethon to raise money for victims of the December 26, 2004, Indian Ocean tsunami. The royal family donates millions of dollars, and a total of $77 million is raised.

*February.* Saudi Arabia holds its first-ever municipal elections. One-third of eligible Saudi men vote in the election. Women are not allowed to run for office or vote.

*August.* King Fahd dies and is succeeded by Crown Prince Abdullah bin Abd al-Aziz Al Saud.

**2006**   *February.* Women vote for the first time in Saudi Arabia.

# BIBLIOGRAPHY

Gold, Dore. *Hatred's Kingdom: How Saudi Arabia Supports the New Global Terrorism.* Washington, D.C.: Regenery Publishing, 2003.

Lippmann, Thomas W. *Inside The Mirage: America's Fragile Partnership with Saudi Arabia.* Boulder, CO: Westview Press, 2004.

Murawiec, Laurent. *Princes of Darkness: The Saudi Assault on the West.* Trans. George Holoch. Lanham, MD: Rowman and Littlefield Publishers, 2005

Schwartz, Stephen. *The Two Faces of Islam: The House of Sa'ud from Tradition to Terror.* New York: Doubleday, 2002.

# FURTHER READING

Aburish, Said K. *The Rise, Corruption, and Coming Fall of the House of Saud.* New York: St. Martin's Press, 1996.

Armstrong, Harold Courtenay. *Lord of Arabia, Ibn Saud: An Intimate Study of a King.* Glen Echo, Maryland: Simon, 2001.

Baer, Robert. *Sleeping with the Devil: How Washington Sold Our Soul for Saudi Crude.* New York: Crown, 2003.

Harper, Robert A. *Modern World Nations: Saudi Arabia.* Philadelphia: Chelsea House, 2002.

Unger, Craig. *House of Bush, House of Saud: The Secret Relationship Between The World's Two Most Powerful Dynasties.* New York: Scribner, 2004.

## WEB SITES

**ArabNet: Saudi, Contents**
www.arab.net/saudi/index.html

**The Royal Embassy of Saudi Arabia (Washington, D.C.)**
www.saudiembassy.net

**Saudi Arabia Information Resource**
www.saudinf.com/index.htm

**The Saudi Network: The Saudi Dynasty**
www.the-saudi.net/al-saud/

**Saudi Strategies: The Al Saud Dynasty**
www.saudistrategies.com/alsaud.html

# PHOTO CREDITS

page:

# INDEX

# About the Authors

**JENNIFER BOND REED** began writing children's stories as a child for her fourth-grade class; little did she know she'd make a career out of it. She has sold over 100 stories and articles to children's magazines. Jennifer is the editor of the e-magazine *Wee Ones* and an instructor for the Institute of Children's Literature. She writes picture-book stories for StoryPlus.com and frequently gives talks and interviews on writing for children and the children's magazine and book industry. She lives in Maryland with her husband, Jeff, and two children, Eric and Emma.

**BRENDA LANGE** has been a journalist, author and public relations professional for 20 years. She graduated summa cum laude from Temple University in Philadelphia and is a member of the American Society of Journalists and Authors. This is the seventh book she has written or revised for Chelsea House.

**ARTHUR M. SCHLESINGER, JR.,** is the leading American historian of our time. He won the Pulitzer Prize for his books *The Age of Jackson* (1945) and *A Thousand Days* (1965), which also won the National Book Award. Professor Schlesinger is the Albert Schweitzer Professor of the Humanities at the City University of New York and has been involved in several other Chelsea House projects, including the series *Revolutionary War Leaders*, *Colonial Leaders*, and *Your Government*.